The Voice that I choose to listen to—the Voice of God's Spirit—speaks loudly and clearly through these pages. And in a Middle Eastern accent! Through these former Muslims, now believers in Christ, the Spirit calls us to live all-out, all-in, with nothing held back—for the glory of God's great name. The men and women who share their stories give powerful encouragement to answer that call and to stand in the fire with them . . . and with Him!

—ANNE GRAHAM LOTZ
INTERNATIONAL SPEAKER
AUTHOR OF *THE DANIEL PRAYER*
CHAIR OF THE NATIONAL DAY OF PRAYER

The call of the Lord Jesus is for His followers to be intentionally courageous. The call of modern culture is for His followers to be increasingly comfortable. *Standing in the Fire* will challenge those of us who are comfortable to envy and emulate our brothers and sisters who are—today—living courageous lives, in service to the King who is worthy of our greatest acts of faith. Tom Doyle reports from the front lines with these stories that expose life that *is* truly life!

—BOB SHANK
FOUNDER, THE MASTER'S PROGRAM
CO-FOUNDER, THE BARNABAS GROUP

We all know about the fire burning in the Middle East. Just turn on the news; you'll hear how that region is exploding, imploding, chaotic, and violent. Please, Christian friend, season your nightly news viewing with this important work from Tom Doyle. Open these pages and fellowship with our brothers and sisters standing in the midst of those flames. They're not just standing; they are boldly advancing the gospel, loving their enemies and winning them to Christ! This book shares both the stories of these bold believers and also practical ways you and I can incorporate some of their hard-won knowledge of walking with Christ. If you will let them, these stories will inspire you to follow Jesus more closely and challenge you to go boldly to those around you who don't yet know Him.

—TODD NETTLETON
HOST, VOM RADIO, THE VOICE OF THE MARTYRS

Once again, Tom Doyle has put a face on the number one issue of the day. No, it's not terrorism but rather, the big news is the spread of the gospel in the Islamic world. Having given their lives to Jesus, these brave believers have faced an enemy that wants them dead. While they may be standing in the fire, these courageous Christians know that one way or another as the prophet Isaiah declared, "Through the fire (they) will not be scorched." Thank you, Tom, for sharing these stories so that we might see the world in a bolder, brighter way because of the good news of the cross.

—JANET PARSHALL
NATIONALLY SYNDICATED TALK SHOW HOST

Tom Doyle unveils compelling true stories from behind the front lines of a great spiritual battle to reveal the heart of God for His people, and their steadfast heart for Him. The faith and courage of these followers of Jesus under extreme persecution is an inspiration and example for us all. We will all benefit to learn, as these valiant Christians have experienced through "relentless trials," that we are not alone, for Jesus is with us, "standing in the fire."

—CURTIS HAIL
PRESIDENT & CEO, E3 PARTNERS MINISTRY / I AM SECOND

Tom Doyle's new book, *Standing in the Fire*, is a fast-paced, inspirational, and at times, very disturbing read. The testimonies of salvation and suffering ring with authenticity and will leave you breathless, tearful, and determined to follow the example of these former Islamic soldiers, who now love Jesus. This book will elevate your faith and propel you to a more committed public stand for the Messiah. I am so grateful that Tom and JoAnn Doyle have sacrificially collected these stories and brought them to us so that we can pray for our brothers and sisters who are regularly facing life-threatening opposition to their faith and ministries.

—DR. MITCH GLASER
PRESIDENT, CHOSEN PEOPLE MINISTRIES

My heart always catches on fire when I read Tom Doyle's stories about the astounding faith and extraordinary love exhibited by believers facing the most intense persecution on earth. Is it possible that God can work so powerfully in such dark and desperate places? *Standing in the Fire* humbles me and inspires me to become more like Jesus. Prepare to have your faith challenged, your heart convicted, and your sleep disrupted. I couldn't put it down.

—CHERYL WEBER
CO-HOST AND INTERNATIONAL PRODUCER, *100 HUNTLEY STREET*

We live in days that call for courageous faith from all who claim to follow Christ. But how do we transition from lives of fear to lives of faith? Tom Doyle and Greg Webster provide the answer in *Standing in the Fire*. The stories will inspire you. But more than that, they will introduce you to flesh-and-blood examples of what it means to courageously live out one's faith. This is a must-read book!

—DR. CHARLES H. DYER
HOST, *THE LAND AND THE BOOK* RADIO PROGRAM
ASSOCIATE PASTOR, GRACE BIBLE CHURCH, SUN CITY, ARIZONA

Standing in the Fire is a timely work; a must-read. Tom Doyle conveys compelling front line stories of courage and conviction from amazing people who daily face death. The American church will surely be inspired as they discover how followers of Jesus can thrive in the midst of staggering persecution, and to long for the time when our Lord will restore completely this fallen world.

—JASON ELAM
NFL ALL-PRO KICKER
DENVER BRONCO RING OF FAME PLAYER

This heart-pounding, page-turner raises your eyes to Jesus and God's passionate pursuit of all people. These true stories helped me to see and pray for Muslims in a new light.

—BRIAN HARDIN
FOUNDER, DAILY AUDIO BIBLE

While we hear of the moving of the Holy Spirit in the Middle East, very few know the actual stories and people whose lives are experiencing the presence of God. By taking us into the lives of these heroes of the faith, *Standing in the Fire* takes us through the veil into the *supernatural*. The Lord not only performed miracles in the past, He is performing modern miracles today. When you finish reading their testimonies, you will not be the same!

—Ray Bentley
Pastor of Maranatha Chapel, San Diego, California
Author of *The Holy Land Key*

STANDING IN THE FIRE

STANDING IN THE FIRE

COURAGEOUS CHRISTIANS LIVING
IN FRIGHTENING TIMES

TOM DOYLE
WITH
GREG WEBSTER

W Publishing Group

An Imprint of Thomas Nelson

Published in Nashville, Tennessee, by W Publishing Group, an imprint of Thomas Nelson. W Publishing and Thomas Nelson are registered trademarks of HarperCollins Christian Publishing, Inc.

Thomas Nelson titles may be purchased in bulk for educational, business, fund-raising, or sales promotional use. For information, please e-mail SpecialMarkets@ThomasNelson.com.

Library of Congress Control Number: 2016917859

ISBN 9780718089214 (eBook)
ISBN 9780718088620 (SC)

Printed in United States of America

18 19 20 LSC 9 8 7 6 5

To Dad.

You're my hero. Watching you I learned what it's like to live courageously, even joyfully, on the front lines. As an FBI agent for more than thirty years, and an organized crime specialist, you never backed down to the Mafia. The other agents admired you and often told me, "Jim Doyle always gets his man." I pray for a generation of believers with the same courage that only Christ can give in the dangerous spiritual arena that we live in today.

CONTENTS

Introduction: Time for a Change in Direction xiii

Chapter 1: The Syrian Firing Squad 1

Chapter 2: There's NO Place Like Homs. 25

Chapter 3: Married to an Imam. 51

Chapter 4: The Muslim Woman at the Well 71

Chapter 5: Just the Usual Damascus Death Threat. . . 91

Chapter 6: The ISIS Recruit from Mosul. 121

Chapter 7: The Secret Police Secret. 141

Chapter 8: The Jerusalem Peace Plan 169

Conclusion 197

Acknowledgments 205

Notes 207

About the Authors 211

INTRODUCTION

Time for a Change in Direction

error-ism. The very word is rooted in fear—mind-numbing, blood-chilling, heart-stopping fear. What could be worse than facing a person dedicated to indiscriminately destroying human life of any kind—men, women, and children? The target of terror can be anybody.

The influences around us—whether news reporters, politicians, or commentators—seem to want nothing more than to deepen our fear of the violent forces in a world that appears to be coming apart at the seams just a bit more each day. In today's world, if we're not careful, we can easily succumb to fear, and when we do, we can become a slave to it. The problem with living in fear is that—besides flying in the face of more than two hundred biblical admonitions to *not* fear—it can cause us to do the very thing we should *not* do. Let me explain.

PRIDE BEFORE THE FALL

My good friend Dan Hansen loves Jesus, and he loves Africa. He's dedicated his life to serving people on the world's second-largest continent. He also loves Africa's backcountry and once told me a fascinating story about lions, roars, and *fear*.

Lions have an especially pernicious way of hunting their prey. It seems that they terrorize their victims into making the worst possible choice about how to protect themselves from being eaten.

The hunt begins when a pack of lions spies a stray animal such as a zebra that has wandered away from its herd, or is sick, or is at the back of the pack. In a remarkable division of labor, male lions line up on one side of the lone animal while lionesses deploy on the opposite side. Once battle lines are in place, the roaring begins.

Male lions possess a singular capacity to discharge a thunderous, spine-chilling roar. In an inevitable fit of terror, the zebra bolts away from the horrific sound—and into the claws of expert killers, the lionesses. Death for the confused victim is certain. If the doomed creature had only understood the real situation, it would have overcome its impulse to flee the noise and instead run *toward* the male lions, who sound like death itself but lack the drive and energy to be the actual killers of the pride's next meal.

We should learn the lesson. The only hope for the zebra is to refuse to run away, and to run *to* the roar.

FEAR FORWARD

Could it be that, for many believers in Christ, the secular news now shapes our outlook on life more than Jesus' words do? We in the West, in particular, seem to have forgotten the Lord's promise: "In the world you will have tribulation; but be of good cheer, I have overcome the world" (John 16:33 NKJV). We have let fear set us running in the wrong direction.

Yet, there are many who live differently. Why? Because they understand who is roaring.

The apostle Peter pinpointed the source: "Your adversary *the devil* prowls around like a roaring lion, seeking someone to devour. Resist him, firm in your faith, knowing that the same kinds of suffering are being experienced by your brotherhood throughout the world" (1 Peter 5:8–9 ESV, emphasis added). *Satan* roars at us from the headlines and the front lines. Yet he is weak and cannot win the fight when believers turn toward him in the power of Christ, the Victor.

The people you'll meet in *Standing in the Fire* are believers who have caught on to the devil's strategy and won't fall for it. They've seen the worst his minions can throw at the world, and they are not leaving the scene, no matter how hot the fire gets. Their courage and faith through unthinkable confrontations with radical Islam is inspiring.

Standing in the Fire is a collection of true accounts of courageous Christians facing down the enemies who appear in today's top news stories. As with my two previous books, *Dreams and Visions* and *Killing Christians*, names, locations, and other identifying details have been changed to protect these current-day heroes of the faith. But their stories are real. So real that you will likely evaluate your own life by comparison, and maybe discover that you have been running in the wrong direction and need to make a U-turn.

Jesus predicted the mess the world is in, so the current state

of things should not really surprise any of us. Christian persecution is at an all-time high. Yet, if you are like me, the reality
continues to shock you.

As a new believer in high school, I fell in love with Jesus and
began to devour His Word. One of my first stops was the book
of Acts. As I read, I envisioned myself as one of the disciples,
spreading the gospel around the known world, and I vividly
remember thinking: *I'm glad the Roman Empire collapsed and we
live in a more civilized world now. Thank You, Lord, that all the
persecution is over and done with.*

But whatever made me think that persecution is off the table?
Jesus clearly promised it to His followers. Even secular news now
regularly covers the growing inhumane treatment of Christians
around the world.

But, as followers of Christ, the message of love He has given
us to take to the world should never be daunted by fear. If it is,
we're running instead of standing.

I believe it's *time for Christ followers to stand firm and no
longer run away*, because our enemy is the one who wants us to
run. During the Babylonian captivity, Meshach, Shadrach, and
Abednego stood confident before King Nebuchadnezzar, whom
they refused to worship, even though he threatened to send them
to a horrifying death. They had no guarantees that God would
intervene.

Yet, just knowing "the God we serve is able to deliver us"
(Dan. 3:17 NIV) was enough for them. And their trust in the
God of Israel, while at the same time having no fear of the king
of the great Babylonian Empire, caused Nebuchadnezzar to lose
it and unravel before their eyes. In a raging fit, he had the three
young Hebrews bound with heavy clothes, tied up, and thrown

into a fire that killed the soldiers who tossed them into the blazing incinerator.

But soon the king would see that the three men were not alone.

Neither are the Jesus followers of today, who right now stand in the fiery furnace of Islamic terrorism in the Middle East. Jesus is with them, and He gives them the reason—and the courage—to stand. They have learned in the fire, and they have much to share with you. Jesus has made available to you the same courage to face down your fears.

Today's world is violent and pitted against those who follow Jesus, and it's not going to change in our lifetime. But we know the end of the story, and in order to live life full throttle for God we must say good-bye to fear and look with hope to the future. After all, Jesus is coming back, and how do you want Him to find you: shaking like a leaf or standing strong in Him, come hell or high water?

In *Killing Christians*, I introduced you to Farid, who lives in Syria in the midst of the world's most feared killing machine, ISIS. Yet, if you met him today, you would be shocked because he appears to live with less stress than you and I do in the relative safety of America. His heart overflows with peace, and a contagious, memorable smile always shines despite his overwhelming adversity.

Farid doesn't merely survive—he *thrives* in Syria. He should be dead by now. Yet, he is not standing alone, and he tells of how he has never felt the presence of Christ more than when he wasn't sure if he would live to see the end of the day. ISIS and other Islamic terrorist groups are stoking the fire perhaps hotter than it has ever been for followers of Christ in the Middle East. Apocalyptic Muslims like ISIS and the regime in Iran hold to an "end-times" scenario, which involves an annihilation of America and Israel. Christians are to be erased if they refuse to convert to Islam.

Recently, Farid told me that thirty threats were spray-painted on the front of his apartment. Terrorists wanted to make sure he got their message. To be sure, he understood the threat, but he stayed, and an astounding array of others are doing the same. You'll meet one of them in our first story. He's a friend of Farid's, and the danger he faced is chilling. In places like Syria, Christians face a fiery furnace.

But Jesus is there, and that's why today's heroes of our faith in the Middle East don't run away in fear. Instead, they *choose* to stay. Despite the cost, they serve God wholeheartedly.

The flames of persecution are blazing. But new heroes of the faith are not afraid, and they are not leaving. Their stories will inspire you, refresh your hope, and show you a way to face your own fears.

The courageous Christians you are about to meet have learned valuable lessons in the midst of their relentless trials. But above all, they have seen time and time again that they are not alone, and will never be, for they are with Jesus, standing in the fire.

> Then King Nebuchadnezzar was astonished; and he rose in haste and spoke, saying to his counselors, "Did we not cast three men bound into the midst of the fire?"
>
> They answered and said to the king, "True, O king."
>
> "Look!" he answered, "I see four men loose, walking in the midst of the fire; and they are not hurt, and the form of the fourth is like the Son of God." (Dan. 3:24–27 NKJV)

1 THE SYRIAN FIRING SQUAD

Osama knew the execution position well—captive kneeling, head bowed slightly forward, hands behind his back. He had led his share of hostages and prisoners to the crest of the sandy hill five miles east of the rebel-held city of Idlib in northern Syria. But this time, he was the one struggling for breath under the black hood cinched tight over his head in the blistering desert sun.

From behind the three members of his firing squad, Commander Mahmoud Ramadan shouted the list of crimes Osama al-Jihadi had committed against Islam. He punctuated each judgment with vicious laughter. Ridicule was standard procedure in the execution of an apostate, and Osama imagined that his cousins on the other side of Idlib could hear the man bellowing. A year earlier, Osama could never have imagined he would be kneeling before an executioner.

The commander's monologue ended abruptly in a single gunshot, and Osama crumpled to the ground. A half dozen rapid-fire shots followed, and blood once again soaked into the sandy hill.

But it was not Osama's.

At precisely 3:00 A.M. one night the previous year, in the basement of a spacious suburban home not far from the bloody mound, a cold-eyed, twenty-ish man raised his hand toward a group of comparably aged males gathered in the underground room. The assembly honored his silent request for their attention.

"When Bashar Al-Assad dies, we will crush the Alawites and slaughter all Christians!" The young man spoke resolutely, confident of his cause.

Jabhat al-Nusra, the Syrian version of al-Qaeda, was now a grim threat to the Bashar Al-Assad regime that had looked so invincible just months before. Still maintaining discretion about its movements, though, the group planned its business a safe forty miles from al-Nusra's primary target, one of the oldest cities in the world. Continually inhabited for more than four thousand years, Aleppo boasts more residents than its slightly older but more well-known sister city and capital, Damascus.

"America will help us overthrow this evil regime. They hate Assad. But *we* are the ones who owe him and his father for what they did to our families in Hama. I will never give up the fight to liberate Syria from this illegitimate infidel. I will die in this fight, because I have no doubt this is what Allah created me for."

The young man returned the nods of his listeners. They, too, hated Assad. The bully of the Levant[1] had too long oppressed them with his massive military and by way of his despicable alliances with Russia and Iran. Shameless flaunting of power only enflamed the hostility against him.

Life was good in Syria—at least for the family of Bashar Al-Assad. The president's wife looked as if she walked into the royal palace straight off of a fashion runway in Paris. The Assads loved the good life in Damascus. President Assad slept well at night—that is, until the Syrian civil war started.

"The one who has the plan for overthrowing the government will speak to you now." The upstart leader smiled and gestured with his right hand toward the basement's side entrance. "You didn't know you would have the pleasure of hearing from our spiritual mentor tonight, did you?"

Fifty men leapt to their feet as Osama al-Jihadi marched through the door and replaced the younger man as the focal point of the room. The straight-backed leader turned powerful shoulders from side to side and surveyed the room for half a minute before speaking.

"So these are my warriors?" The hint of a smile crossed Osama's face. "I like what I see—not only in this room but also in Syria's future. We will take what is rightfully ours as Sunni Muslims. We outnumber Assad and the filthy Alawites nearly five to one.

"So tell me, how have we let this trifling Alawite tumor control us for so long? How can *he* cause us to live as exiles in our own country?" Osama glared at his audience.

"I'll tell you how: it's because cowards have led us! But those days are over. Many of us here will die in this holy fight. But by Allah's strength, *so will Bashar Al-Assad*. We will see that he gets what is coming to him."

Osama al-Jihadi stood motionless. His eyes shifted from cohort to cohort until he had personally acknowledged nearly every man in the room. Finally, he nodded toward the one who had introduced him, and the meeting was over.

Jamal al-Jihadi filed slowly out of the basement with the

other men but briefly caught his older cousin's steady eye. He smiled and bowed his head toward his leader and uncle's son. The strong man of al-Nusra had no idea that every time his favorite cousin grinned, he was praying for Osama.

"Jamal, you have to get out! My sister in Lebanon is ready for us." Jamal's fiery wife, Safa, slammed both hands flat on the kitchen table, her words and eyes pleading with the man seated across from her. "I don't care if Osama is your cousin. You're playing with fire. Surely he suspects something. Osama recruited you, so the two of you could be 'freedom fighters.' But these people of his are nothing but cold-blooded terrorists. How can you even go to the meetings anymore in good conscience? You're a believer!"

Jamal closed his eyes, sincerely considering the fears of the wife he so adored—and the mother of his three young children. Barely five feet tall, his lovable stick of dynamite was also by far the best cook in either of their extended families. Her Lebanese heritage added literal and figurative spice to every family gathering.

Their passionate dialogue had begun the instant he entered the kitchen, groggy from too little sleep after the late-night meeting. Jamal mainly listened, and after just ten minutes, he felt as if the talk with his wife had been in progress for hours.

He picked up a serving dish from the center of the table and scraped the last fava beans onto a piece of pita. Studying the pale green objects, he smiled softly, and raised his hand like a schoolboy waiting to be called on at the madrassa.[2]

"I would like to say something."

Safa accepted the interruption and with flair slapped her right hand across her mouth.

"My dear Safa, when Jesus came into my life, I knew He called me first to our precious family, yet my heart is in agony for my larger al-Jihadi family as well. Some people are called to take Jesus to foreign lands, but I'm to stay here. This is my calling. It begins for me in my house, but I am willing to tell everyone else about Him too."

"Yes, I know that, Jamal, and I love you for being such a brave man. But you were raised a Muslim—we both were—and your family is involved in *terrorism*. Many of them are! Do you think they will not notice the change in you? It's all over your face. The Holy Spirit has marked you. Please let someone else reach out to Osama—anyone but you!

"We may play the game in front of them, but I'm telling you, somehow they know what's happened to you. Somehow, someway they *know*! And besides, Sharia law is a cruel master, and I just don't think I can take it anymore. Please, can we go to Lebanon?"

"My love." Jamal shook his head almost imperceptibly. "I promise you . . . they don't know. Not even Osama. We have been best friends since I was five. I love him like a brother. I know everything about him, and he knows everything about me—except the most important thing. But that is coming soon.

"When he believes, we will have a modern-day Paul. Something good will come out of Syria. When Osama accepts our Lord, he will shake the world. I feel this in my heart."

Jamal pushed back from the table and crossed his legs. "How are the children this morning?"

Safa scowled. "Jamal, habibi,[3] you are very good at changing the subject when I have you cornered. And don't 'remind' me that you've had lots of practice either!"

"Of course not, my love. Let me conclude our conversation properly." Jamal smiled broadly at his spritely bride. "This was a wonderful breakfast."

Jamal slowly coiled the black hose of a *nargila* (hookah) onto the floor between them. Osama rested his cup of intensely black Arabic coffee on his right knee and with his left hand reached for the mouthpiece Jamal had just relinquished. Well into their third cup of coffee, the cousins neared the end of a long night of deep conversation. The exchange with Safa that morning played in the back of Jamal's mind, but he determined that his wife's legitimate fears would not stop him from doing what he could to bring his cousin into God's light.

Jamal cradled the coffee cup in both hands. His eyes drifted up to his companion. "Osama, you are a great leader. But do you ever worry about the future? I mean, for your family? Honestly, do you?"

Osama looked at Jamal as if he had not quite understood the question.

"Osama. When Assad is gone for good, what next?"

The older cousin nodded. Excitement flitted in his eyes. "Israel, of course." He smiled at Jamal. "And, no, I don't worry—because we will win. We *have* to win this war, no matter how long it takes. There is no other way this can end, Jamal. It may take ten more years, but losing is not an option. Our families will be slaughtered if we fail."

Osama paused, considering his next words. "So, to be clear:

I suppose from time to time I do worry about my children, and especially my sons. Our evil president will no doubt try to kill them all. Yes . . . that part does worry me."

Energy drained from Osama's face, and expressionless eyes focused on his friend and cousin. "That's why we're fighting, Jamal. It may be for Syria, but it is also for our families who will have the best life possible when we defeat this contemptible Assad regime once and for all. When we're done, we'll make sure there will be no heir to ever challenge us. Syria will be a Sunni-led country again, and once we join with Iraq, we will be strong enough to level Israel. My family—*our* family—used to enjoy vacations in the Golan. And now the filthy Jews have had it for far too long! That must end."

Osama paused to sip his coffee. "Jamal, one of my goals in life is to see the Assad family suffer a slow death. Won't that be pure joy for us? Can you imagine watching him die just like Khadafy did? Justice *is* coming."

Jamal stared at his cousin in silence for several seconds. "Actually, Osama: No, I can't imagine that." Jamal looked down at his cup of black liquid.

Osama watched as his cousin drank the last of his coffee, but said nothing more until he bid Jamal good-bye at the front door. Before stepping through the courtyard gate of Osama's house, Jamal checked the street and surrounding rooftops several times for movement. Al-Nusra had secured the neighborhood last month, but the Syrian Army infiltrated every so often, which meant that death by sniper fire was possible at any time.

Well past midnight, Jamal entered his kitchen through the back door. Finding the light on, he had hoped Safa was still up, cooking, but he discovered her asleep in their bedroom. Jamal undressed, pulled a sleeping shirt over his head, and slipped into bed beside his wife. As he slid his right hand past the curve of Safa's hip and around her waist, she startled and sat up. Her eyes found Jamal's form in the mostly dark room.

"Is everything all right, Jamal? How was Osama? Did he start screaming about Assad or Israel again?"

Jamal reached for Safa's hand. "Maybe you're right about him, Safa. He has so much hate in his heart. When he started to talk about seeing Assad die a slow death tonight, something sinister took over. The evil in his eyes truly scared me. I've seen it in his speeches to al-Nusra recruits as well.

"If he knew my secret, that evil would consume me in an instant. He is *ruled* by hate." Jamal paused, and then whispered, mostly to himself. "How long can I keep up this game? Lord, we need a miracle."

Safa leaned toward her husband and laid her head softly on his chest. The two Jesus followers drifted to sleep in each other's arms.

Shock waves nearly threw Jamal to the floor. Instantly awake, he heard Safa gasp as he jerked upright beside their bed. The explosion couldn't have been more than a block away.

Are the children okay? His mind raced through the possibilities. *Was it the Syrian Army? The Americans? Russia?*

Three al-Jihadi children sprinted into their parents' room and scrambled under the bedcovers. A smaller noise focused Jamal's attention. His cell phone was ringing. A second later, Safa's added its familiar notes. Safa flicked on the bedside light just as Jamal fished a cell phone from the pocket of pants he had left on the floor.

As he answered, a familiar voice—one of the men from al-Nusra—blurted at Jamal, "It's Osama!"

"Osama? Is he dead?"

At the word "dead," Safa froze. She gave up looking for her phone and stared at Jamal.

"Okay. How bad is he hurt?" Jamal's eyes scanned the room, looking at nothing. "Where did it land? Are Amal and the children safe?" He paused again for an answer. "I'll be right there."

Jamal squinted past the blinding red lights flashing beside the courtyard entrance he had walked through on his way home four hours earlier. With each red pulse, he could see that little remained of the entry portion of Osama's house. Jamal darted up to the ambulance just as two paramedics lifted a stretcher through the open back doors of the white van.

"Where will you take him?" Jamal screamed. He had maintained control of his emotions until the moment he spotted his cousin and best friend under the blood-soaked sheet.

"The al-Watani hospital." The lead attendant spoke as he jumped into the van and pulled the stretcher on board.

Jamal looked at Osama and read the agony in his barely open eyes. The younger man forced a smile and prayed silently, *Lord, is this it for Osama?* As the ambulance door slammed shut, Jamal wondered if he would ever again see his cousin and best friend alive.

Although surgery to remove shrapnel and stop internal bleeding should have taken no longer than two hours, four hours later, the al-Jihadi family sat in the al-Watani hospital waiting room with no word from medical personnel on Osama's condition. Jamal had a bad feeling.

Osama al-Jihadi's wife, Amal, sat at the center of a circle of ten women. Tears spilled down the front of her niqab.[4]

Jamal stood outside the group of black-clad females, listening as Amal choked out her fears. "I've dreamed that Osama would soon be dead. I wake up crying almost every night. I think he is cursed and condemned to die already."

The two women closest to Amal—her sisters—each touched one of the sobbing woman's shoulders, as a voice from across the room called out, "Are you Osama al-Jihadi's wife?"

Amal stood slowly, braced on each side by the two sisters, prepared to receive the feared news, and turned toward the voice. A man in surgical clothes stood in the doorway of the waiting room.

"Osama survived the surgery and has been moved to intensive care. There was more damage internally than we picked up on the X-ray. He has many injuries and an infection. If it goes septic, he could easily die. Even if he makes it through the next few days, he will be here for several weeks, perhaps a month." The man in green shrugged. "Maybe more. I am sorry. We had the best doctors in the area, and his case was challenging even for them. Osama is in a medically induced coma to stabilize him. We can thank Allah that he is alive."

Amal howled, and her black form crumpled toward her sisters. The woman's body slipped through their arms, and the two helpers, caught off guard by Amal's faint, managed only to soften her drop to the floor.

Amal revived and, unhurt from her fall, stayed with Osama that night and through the next two days. When she at last broke from keeping watch beside her husband, Jamal took her place in the hospital room. He sat alone next to Osama. A handful of nurses came and went, ignoring Jamal, and for nearly an hour, he said nothing. Finally, he leaned close to his comrade's ear and spoke quietly.

"I kick myself that I never told you. Here you are in a coma, and no one knows if you will survive or not. Your house is destroyed, Osama, but at least Amal and your children are safe in my home. Safa cooks all day, and there is much noise in the house. You should see it, Osama."

Jamal paused and covered his face with his hands before continuing.

"Well, I know you can't hear me, but here I go." He laid his left forearm on the bed beside the comatose figure.

"Osama, I began following Jesus last year. I found a Bible, and I could not put it down. I don't even know where I got it. Initially, I wanted to find out where it had been corrupted. Every night in bed, I read under the covers by the light of my phone. I waited until after Safa was asleep, and sometimes I would not even sleep myself. But that didn't matter. This Jesus was more than I could handle, Osama. I mean He *loved* people who were suffering—little children, the helpless, the marginalized, and the poor. He took time for people—*especially* the *sinners*. The worst ones were drawn to Him, and He never turned them away. Did you know Jesus caused such a stir that news about Him traveled all the way *to Syria* from Israel?" He paused, suppressing the urge to feel foolish at talking so intimately with an all-but-dead body, then pushed on.

"Seeing this loving Jesus, I had to come to grips with the depths of hate in my heart. I realized it was an acid destroying me on the inside. And then I read where Jesus said, 'Love your enemies.' This made no sense to me at all. *Is Jesus majnoon?*[5] I wondered. That sort of thinking in the Middle East is ludicrous.

"This is what I could not shake, though: His message of love. Even sinners could receive Jesus' love. In fact, the *only* people Jesus condemned were the religious people who weren't living the way they forced others to. And I asked myself, *Are the Pharisees Muslim imams in disguise?* They are so similar!

"So, Osama, I have my Bible, and every time I come to see you I'm going to read it to you. I'll start now . . . 'I have come that they might have life—'"

"And that they might have it more abundantly."

Jamal's head jerked toward the door at the sound of another man's voice.

"My apologies if I startled you. You may remember me— Dr. Ahmad. I didn't know you were a believer, Jamal. When did this happen?"

Jamal stood up. "Of course I remember you! When my father died in this hospital, you were remarkably kind to him—and to us. To answer your question: I haven't exactly told my family yet . . . other than my wife."

The doctor nodded, smiling. "Join the club. Not exactly the safest message to be spreading around Syria these days, is it? But we can pray, and we can slowly draw people into their need for Jesus. Today people are empty inside. They walk down the streets like robots without any emotion."

Relief washed over Jamal that his secret was safe with at least one other person. He listened as Dr. Ahmad became more animated.

"How much more killing can we take? Religion is just a dead-end street. You work so hard to keep the rules, and for what reason?" Ahmad shook his head. "I wasn't any closer to God—even though I made the Hajj![6] I've lived here my whole life, and I have never had inner peace like I received as a gift from heaven when I gave myself to Jesus. My family soon followed, but, of course, we have to keep that to ourselves. Our secrets are safe between us, right, Jamal?" The doctor paused again, formulating his next words.

"Can I ask you a question?"

Jamal nodded. "Sure."

"Your cousin is one of the most feared men in this region. Jabhat al-Nusra has leveled villages and instituted Sharia law. Do you not find it remarkable that Jesus called *you* to reach him? Who would he listen to, other than you, his best friend and cousin? Do you think he is open to anything about Jesus?"

Jamal looked at the floor. "I really don't know. I was hoping to . . ." He choked on his words. "I wanted to tell him . . ."

Dr. Ahmad rested a hand on Jamal's shoulder as tears dripped from Jamal's face to the tile floor.

"Jamal, if Osama survives, let's both tell him. We may live in Syria, but it's time to be bold. Am I right, or am I wrong?"

Jamal brushed his cheek with his right hand and looked this fellow believer in the eye.

Dr. Ahmad took Jamal's cue. "Yes! We can do this together. Agreed?"

"Agreed! Now we must pray. And perhaps you heard me when you came in the room: My goal is to read the New Testament to Osama every time I'm here."

For the next two and a half weeks, Jamal visited Osama each day. He read most of the New Testament to his cousin.

"Safa!" Jamal turned his face from the cell phone and nearly shouted at his wife, beside him in the front seat of their car. "It's Dr. Ahmad!"

He listened again to the voice on the phone.

"Jamal, he's awake! I found Amal eating lunch in the waiting room with the children, but she is now with Osama. He's alert, asking questions, and is quite emotional. Can you come down here right away?"

"I'm actually on my way to the hospital right now, and Safa is with me."

Syrian artillery had renewed its abuse of Idlib that morning, and Jamal raced through the streets, avoiding the seemingly random explosions only by God's grace. When he and Safa finally scurried into Osama's hospital room, the first words from the man in the bed astounded him.

"Jamal! My wonderful cousin! Thank you for coming to see me so many times."

Jamal walked slowly to the bed. "But, Osama, how did you know? Did Amal tell you I'd been here?"

"No. She didn't have to. I often heard you. You prayed over me, and the words you read were like nothing I've ever heard before. I want to hear more." Osama grinned at his younger cousin.

That night, Jamal and Safa knelt in their living room, bent forward with their faces touching the floor, and prayed for Osama. Thirty minutes into their prayer vigil, Jamal straightened up and opened his eyes. Safa sensed the change in her husband's position and raised her face from the floor. She looked at Jamal, trying to read his thoughts.

"This is *face time*, habibti."[7] Jamal chuckled. "It's the real thing, not just what we do these days instead of connecting with someone online or over the phone. I can imagine that true believers have been doing this for centuries when they plead with the God of heaven to intervene in some special way."

Jamal raised his eyes and arms toward the ceiling. "Lord, we call on Your name, for Osama!"

The next day, Jamal joined Osama again at the hospital. No longer in ICU, Osama now had more time to himself, with fewer medical staff hovering around. Alone with only Jamal, Osama hungered for more information from his cousin about what he had heard during the coma.

"The words were from the Bible, Osama. It is the true Word of God, and that's why I read it to you." Jamal watched to see if Osama would flinch at his explanation. "The very words of God contain life. And when *I* first read them, I felt complete inner peace for *the first time in my life*." Jamal paused again. "You know, as I do, that the Bible is considered a holy book by the religion we were raised in."

Osama cocked his head. "What do you mean, 'the religion we were raised in'?"

Eying the man in the hospital bed, Jamal drew a long breath and continued, "Osama, I gave up religion . . . a while ago. I follow Jesus now." There, he had said it and wouldn't—couldn't—retreat. "The more I studied Islam back when I was preparing to be an imam, the more questions I had. But they were never answered by our clerics. I was ridiculed, sometimes even beaten, just for asking them.

"Yet Jesus said, 'Ask, and it shall be given to you. Seek, and you will find. Knock, and it will be opened to you.' He *welcomes* questions, and His answers are . . . amazing.

"Osama, this book—the Bible—will turn your life around. I know you could have me killed for talking to you like this, but, my dear cousin, I challenge *you* to read it too. It will change everything."

Osama's face hardened briefly. "I don't want change. I am happy the way I am."

"What do you mean by that?"

Osama ignored the challenge. "Jamal, reading the Bible here is out of the question. What if someone sees me?"

Jamal smirked. "Are you *afraid*, Osama? Afraid someone might object? Afraid I might be right? This is new for me to see you—"

Osama cut him off. "No! I am *not* afraid! I will do whatever I want." His eyes narrowed. Then he continued quietly. "I will read the Bible for myself."

Jamal nodded but said no more. He had what he wanted. The two men sat in silence for several minutes until Jamal stood up abruptly, kissed his cousin on both cheeks, and left the hospital room.

That evening, Jamal and Safa fed the children an early

supper, tucked them in bed, and spent several hours praying for Osama's Bible-reading time. The husband-wife team agreed to fast on behalf of the al-Nusra leader.

For ten days, Osama remained in bed and did nothing for entertainment except read the Bible Jamal had given him. Jabhat al-Nusra members had begun once again to visit, and each time, he slipped the Bible under his pillow.

Well into his second week of Scripture reading, Osama returned to the Gospels. *What would it profit a man to gain the whole world and forfeit his soul?* This time, the words from Mark 8 shot through Osama's heart, and he could not read on.

Osama laid the open book facedown on his chest, closed his eyes, and spoke softly. "I don't want to forfeit my soul. What does this mean? The words haunt me. Give me a sign, Jesus, if You're real."

A voice interrupted Osama's prayer.

"Good morning, Osama. I must say that you have improved dramatically in the last week."

The patient opened his eyes. "Marhaba,[8] Dr. Ahmad!"

The physician stepped close to his patient's bedside. "Osama, you've been on a long road, but I'm happy to say you will be released soon." He glanced at the floor, then looked his patient in the eye. "You have been given a second chance at life. We thought we might lose you when you were brought here after the bombing, but *He* has a path for you. Seek, and you will find it.

"Soon, you will no doubt be called back into this dreadful war. Al-Nusra is waiting for you, but I wonder, how long can the city be held with all the foreign invaders that have gotten involved?

"Now, here is your physician's prescription for full health. My recommendation is for the long run, Osama. I ask you: 'What would it profit a man to gain the whole world and forfeit his soul?'"

Ahmad couldn't interpret the stunned expression on Osama's face but sensed he had said enough. The surgeon touched his patient's right arm, then turned and walked out of the room. Osama stared after the doctor, paralyzed by his final sentence. Six words formed in his mind: *I have to talk to Jamal.*

Three months later, familiar faces surrounded Osama once again at a meeting of the Jabhat al-Nusra. It was the third day in a row the group had assembled, but Osama no longer stood at the front of the room. He was not in charge of this meeting.

Osama sagged in a chair circled by a dozen men, including the young man who once felt pride in his job of introducing Osama for a surprise appearance. Half dead from nearly three full days of beatings, Osama prayed silently that his newfound Lord would simply take his life.

Jesus, keep dear Amal, and my children safe in Lebanon. Please keep the al-Nusra killers from finding them. And thank You for Safa and Jamal. Oh, how You used them to rescue me. I will not deny You, Jesus. You have my word on that.

Rahman al-Awani, the new group leader, spat out a command, interrupting Osama's thoughts. Two thugs wrestled Osama from the chair and dragged him down a dank hallway. They slammed him, face down, on the floor by an office door.

The commander stepped close and bent over. "This can all end today, Osama," he hissed at the prisoner. "And I don't mean your death. Tell me who gave you the Bible and give up this foolish, treacherous conversion story of yours. Say the Shahada,[9] and freedom can be yours again.

"Oh, and how it would benefit others! Surely you don't want anything to happen to your family in the Druze village where they're hiding in Lebanon, do you? Rashaya is not very far from here, you know. Would you rather see them yourself, or should *we* pay them a visit?"

Osama opened his left eye and cocked his head up, in the direction of Rahman's voice. He whispered his answer. "I do not accept your offer. You can kill me, but I will not deny Jesus."

An hour later, Osama drifted into consciousness. He had passed out after being deposited on the floor of a prison cell, but now another voice he did not know was speaking to him. The smell of cigarette smoke helped Osama determine the direction the sound came from. Someone in the hall outside his cell was smoking and talking to him. The man seemed to be preparing some sort of proposal for the prisoner.

Mahmoud Ramadan leaned his back against the wall just beyond Osama's range of view from the cell. "I must say I'm impressed by your faith. I have learned from you, and I sometimes wonder if you are persuading me." The voice paused to drag on his cigarette. "You were a rising leader in al-Nusra, and you threw it all away for *Him*. Why did you even tell them in the first place about leaving Islam?

"I cannot say that I have ever seen this much resolve in a man. With the beatings you've been given, a typical prisoner would confess to anything we charge them with. What's more: we *need* you, Osama. Now that Russia has entered the war, we cannot spare even one leader, especially one with your abilities and influence.

"All you have to do is say the words. You don't even have to believe them in your heart. Just say it. Confess that you have returned to Islam. I'll even tell them that you've reconsidered. Don't you see? I'm trying to help you and—of course you know—this could get me killed. But I see something in you I admire. Please, Osama, just say the words."

The monologue seemed to be over. The man's silence suggested that it was Osama's turn to speak.

"I won't deny my Savior who did not deny me. I won't deny Him in my heart. And I won't deny Him with my lips."

The man outside let a dozen seconds pass before speaking again. "Osama, do you even know who I am? Let me tell you. I'm the man in charge of your firing squad tomorrow. Your execution is scheduled for 8:00 A.M. You have no more chances. But . . ." The voice paused and a new wave of smoke filtered into Osama's cell. "This is how it will go: Tomorrow you will be taken in a van to the execution site outside of Idlib. You're familiar with it, aren't you?"

Osama nodded, and then said, "Yes, I've been there." The scene of executions he had administered flitted through his mind.

"After you're put in the death position, I will say a few words. When you hear the first shot—it will miss you—hit the ground like a dead man and *do not move*. Do not move a muscle in your body, and breathe shallow breaths.

"When you hear the van drive away, take off your mask, get up, and walk east. Within a few miles, you will come to the Syrian Army. Hold up your arms toward the lookout hill and surrender. They will not kill you."

Osama let the man's words register. "Why are you . . . how can you do this?"

No one answered. The voice was gone.

At 7:35 the next morning, Rahman al-Awani stood in the doorway of Osama's prison cell, relishing the chance to mock him one more time. "You are foolish, and what a pity to think of what will happen to your family now!"

Osama faced his captor but did not listen to the words. His mind raced with questions: *Who is the captain of the squad? Why would he favor me? Will he really do as he said?*

He heard Rahman's final, terse words: "Take him away."

As he stumbled out of the van and marched to the crest of the hill, black hood in place over his head, Osama could see nothing, but the stench of death and rotted blood told him where he was. The voice from his prison encounter the night before—much louder now—railed at the prisoner, laughing maniacally as he read the charges against *the Christian*. Osama still wondered if Mahmoud Ramadan would follow through. His theatrics—if that's what they were—sounded convincing.

For me, to live is Christ, thought Osama, *and to die is . . .*

A single shot from an AK-47 stopped his silent proclamation. Osama crumpled to the ground . . . just as he was told.

A WORD FROM OSAMA

I never saw Mahmoud Ramadan's face because his plan worked exactly as he said it would. After the first shot, I heard several more. I continued to lie still until I heard the van drive away. At that point, I rose up, looked around, and saw the other members of the firing squad lying dead around me. I hadn't realized that he planned to kill them so I could go free. He risked everything to save me, and my heart breaks for the lost men he killed so I could live. They have families and were just following orders.

I fled the scene of the execution and surrendered to the Syrian Army stationed several miles away. After questioning me for two days, they set me free! I was astounded and still cannot understand why, other than that God did a miracle. Even this, though, is just one of many. That I am alive after the bombing of my home, the life-and-death surgery, my commitment to follow Jesus, the beatings, and the firing squad—all say that God is using me. His miracles keep me alive until my work here is complete—whenever that may be.

For the moment, I am safe in a monastery in Syria. I spend my days memorizing verses and chapters of the New Testament and praying for my family, who are still alive and well in Lebanon. Although they now know I am safe, for several days they endured the pain of thinking I had been executed.

I called Amal when I arrived at the monastery, but when she heard my voice, she couldn't say a word. Jamal and Safa were with her, and Jamal took the phone from her.

"My dear cousin, I am alive," was all I said.

I think he wondered if my call was a dream, but then the shouts of celebration from everyone with Jamal were so loud, I thought they would wake up their whole village. Even before my "execution," they knew I had been in trouble.

After I began following Jesus, Jabhat al-Nusra came to find me. I had failed to show up for meetings, and they suspected I was a traitor of some sort. They took me prisoner, but not before I convinced Amal and my children of Jesus' love.

My family had spent weeks trying to comprehend the transformation in my life. My love for them had changed, and they could tell. I asked Amal to forgive me for how I had treated her not like a wife but more like a servant to meet my every need. I began to love her with the love I had experienced from Jesus, and, thanks be to Him, she could not turn that down.

I long to see her, my children, Jamal, and Safa, of course, but for now it is not safe for me to travel in Syria, let alone try to get to Lebanon. When others from al-Nusra arrived at the execution site and found the bodies of the firing squad, they went on a manhunt to find me, assuming that somehow I was responsible for the deaths.

There's also another reason I'm not yet ready to leave Syria. I have some unfinished business. Somehow I must meet the man I have never seen. Before I go anywhere else, I have to find Mahmoud Ramadan.

A WORD ABOUT OSAMA

Jesus has given Syrian believers fresh hope because of Osama. His transformation shows how much Jesus loves us and that He has not forgotten us.

Osama was willing to die, even though he began following Jesus only a couple of months before his arrest. His life makes us answer a question I ask myself every day, and I think all believers should do the same: "Am I ready to die for Jesus?" He did not even try to hide from Jabhat al-Nusra although its following of Sharia law is every bit as diabolical as ISIS. Osama knew word of his conversion would reach his al-Nusra followers, and they would come for him. It's not an exaggeration to say that the group's favorite entertainment is to tor-ture victims while reciting Suras from the Quran. But Jesus in Osama was more than a match for them.

Osama al-Jihadi is my new hero of the faith.

—Farid Assad from *Killing Christians'* "The Only Empty Graveyard in Syria"

2 THERE'S NO PLACE LIKE HOMS

Two men walked soberly atop the fifty-foot-high inner walls of Krak des Chevaliers, interrupting their prayers every few minutes to scan the green slopes dropping away toward the west bank of the Orontes River two thousand feet below. Built by Crusaders, the limestone castle under their feet, bleached light gray by nine hundred years of Syrian Desert sun, blazed in the afternoon light, its precision ashlar facing still a wonder to twenty-first-century archaeologists.

Farid Assad[1] looked at his longtime prayer partner, friend, and fellow pastor who stood gazing into the Homs Gap valley below. Strategically critical during most of Middle East history, through it likely poured the twenty thousand soldiers of King Hadadezer of Zobah[2] on their way to destroy Israel's King David. But the Hebrew giant-killer crushed the invaders and subjected all of Syria to his rule.

We could use another King David about now. The man known as Pastor Joseph smiled at the thought and turned his head from the cliffside leading to the Silk Road below to look at his friend. Treasuring their time together before confronting the chaos of

Homs, twenty-five miles to the west, they had been praying for nearly two hours. The pair of itinerant pastors feared the last forty-eight hours of their nearly three-week circuit to Syrian house churches would be their most difficult.

"When my dad pastored the Baptist church, we were always in danger, but now I wonder if there are any believers at all left in Homs." A stiff afternoon breeze swept Farid's voice into the open space surrounding the Jebel Kalakh.[3]

"I fear there are none. My father's church is no longer standing; it's a pile of rubble. Julia Restaurant where we used to celebrate family birthdays is gone. I proposed to Rima at the Old Clock Square. The tower is still standing, but the clock is gone." He raised his eyebrows. "How symbolic! The city's been beaten down by the Israelites, Alexander the Great, Romans, Crusaders, and always survived, but now . . . I wonder if time has finally run out for Homs."

Farid shook his head. "The street I lived on is erased too. Joseph, did you see the YouTube drone video of Homs? I cried when I watched it. Three-fourths of the city has been obliterated. I'm afraid I'll cry again when I see it in person. This may be the last time we walk the streets of our sweet city."

Farid pointed toward the valley. "We'd better go. The cease-fire won't hold for long. Are you ready?" Joseph looked down at the castle's outer wall a dozen yards below them and nodded solemnly.

The parking area at the base of the citadel was empty except for Pastor Joseph's 1970 Mercedes Benz. Multiple repairs through years of hard use resulted in doors, hood, roof, and trunk that sported four different colors. As Farid and Joseph settled into the rugged sedan, Farid's phone lit up.

Joseph started the car and sighed. "You get more death threats than most people get mail. Did you just get another one?"

The weekly flood of e-mail peaked on Friday afternoon following midday prayers. Noontime prayers at the mosque routinely launched local fanatics into a frenzy of hate. But none of Farid's tormentors surpassed Rashid Abbas for persistence and vitriol. A serious repeat offender, he'd been threatening Farid for five years. This late-breaking text message was Rashid Abbas with his current warning. Farid winced and set his aging cell phone facedown on the console between the front seats.

Joseph eyed the scratches on the back of Farid's flip phone and laughed. "Farid! You've got to get a new cell phone! I've lived in Syria all of my life, so I'm fascinated with ancient artifacts, but not ones I use to call people on."

Tension drained from Farid's face. He picked up the phone again, flicked it open, and turned the face toward Joseph.

The pastor frowned. "You saved Rashid Abbas's contact information? He wants to kill you! Why give him the time of day?"

"When he calls," Farid explained, "it reminds me to pray for him. I figure nobody else will, so he's the number one terrorist on my prayer list. What I wonder is: Why doesn't he just kill me? He's had plenty of opportunities."

Joseph scratched his head and nodded. "Given how often he calls, he certainly is getting well covered in prayer."

"Yeah. I suppose."

As the highway curved southwest, Farid squinted out the window and across the fields, trying to make out the border with Lebanon. The two men rode in silence for several minutes before Farid spoke again.

"Joseph, do you remember all the jokes about Homs? The city gained quite a reputation. Everyone in Syria seemed to know the latest Homs story. I even heard a few Homs jokes while I was in Lebanon and Jordan. Our American friend Julia said they reminded her of blonde jokes in the States.

"But Homs had some of the most hospitable people in our entire country!" He rested his forehead against the car window. "I wonder what happened to *them*."

At the city-center traffic circle thirty minutes later, the multi-colored Mercedes turned east and headed along Hamidiyah Street. After several blocks, Joseph parked the car where the face of a three-story apartment building had collapsed into the road. The two pastors continued on foot, climbing through the wreckage of what had been a neighborhood. Dozens of former residents stumbled zombie-like along the rubble-bound streets, scavenging for edibles or anything of value. The Old City looked as if it had been nuked.

Joseph and Farid turned left at the intersection with Alquzon Street. Farid scrambled over a four-foot-high pile of debris and stopped. He peered into the late-afternoon shadows, unable to believe his eyes. Without a word, he leaned forward and sobbed.

Joseph gaped at the devastation while, without raising his head, Farid pointed down the street. "That pile of cement and bricks. . . ." His words came out in a whisper. "It's our church, Joseph. We met Jesus there. Remember the day we were baptized together? You were twelve, and I was ten."

Joseph crouched to put his arm around Farid and spoke slowly. "How could I forget that day? People in the church saw the fire we had for Jesus even at a young age. I loved it when they called us James and John—the Sons of Thunder. Most Syrian boys wanted to grow up and play soccer for Barcelona." He patted Farid's shoulder. "We wanted to be apostles."

The "Christian section" of Homs lay in ruins. Farid and Joseph walked through the rubble for a quarter of an hour, stunned by the gravity of the loss. They stopped periodically to ponder the remains of one church after another.

"Farid, who would've ever thought our city would end up looking like this? I've seen pictures of Dresden, Germany, after World War II, and Homs looks worse. These buildings—what's left of them—are just brick and mortar, but think of the thousands of ruined lives they represent.

"Third-largest city in Syria." Joseph's voice trailed off. He raised his hands toward the destruction around them. "*Stable* and *secure*. That's what we used to think of Homs. We and the 750,000 others who used to live here. Supposedly, the population is less than 200,000 now. To look around us, you'd think we'd had an earthquake of unimaginable proportions." Joseph laughed grimly. "A six-year-long earthquake."

Farid listened quietly, working to hold back more tears.

"The fault line runs straight through Homs, and now the sheep have scattered."

At first, Christians were simply caught in the crossfire of the Syrian government's war against the Sunnis. The real terror began when the Islamic State took over the Sunni resistance. Tremors that began with a simple protest against President Assad resulted in political and human loss off the Richter scale.

STANDING IN THE FIRE

"No wonder the believers left," Farid whispered. "Did you see the pictures? ISIS lined up the men and executed them in front of their families. It looked like it was on this very street. Then those five men wearing orange jumpsuits were killed one right after another just outside Homs, exactly like the Egyptian massacre on the beach in Libya.

"Joseph." Farid looked thoughtfully at his fellow pastor. "I'm thankful we bought a place to be buried. We may yet need it. If anyone ever doubted there was a God, though, I challenge him or her to explain how we are still alive! Two pastors like us who live to tell Syrians about Jesus, and our *graveyard is still empty?* Only Jesus could pull that off."

Farid folded his arms. "The Islamic State, Jabhat al-Nusra, and Druze leaders have all threatened to kill us. And since the war started, the Alawites have even become vicious. Now they want to kill us too—like our friend Rashid." He nodded toward Joseph. "But Jesus has us in the palm of His hand."

"Plus the other twenty-three men who bought the graveyard with us," Joseph added. "They're still alive, even though they're committed to die for Jesus in Syria if need be."

Farid's phone rang. Rashid Abbas again.

"Are you going to answer it?"

Farid's eyes drifted up from the phone and gazed down the street. He straightened his shoulders. "No . . . No, I'm not going to answer his phone call. I'm going to answer him in person. He lives just around the corner." Farid swung his head to look Joseph in the eye. "Would you care to join me for tea with Rashid?"

Joseph returned the look. "You want to visit the man who promises to kill you?"

"I do." Farid stepped around a block of concrete and began

walking down the street. He called back to Joseph, "And I even have a gift for him!"

As his friend's intent registered, a baffled Joseph followed Farid around the street corner.

"Thank you, Um Walid. The cookies are delicious. We needed the tea, and your hospitality is much appreciated." Farid nodded at Rashid's wife.

"Farid and Joseph."

The two men turned toward the voice.

"You are both welcome in my home anytime." Rashid Abbas entered the room and shook hands vigorously with the two Christians. "What can I help you with?"

Joseph sat straight on the couch and cleared his throat, choosing his words. "Is there something my friend has done to offend you, Rashid? Your calls and texts are terribly threatening. He says you tell him that Christians are the reason Syria is at war. Do you actually believe Christians started this conflict?"

Farid watched Rashid's reaction to Joseph's question and tried not to let his enthusiasm show. He had long wondered if Rashid would admit to threatening him or mask the warnings with typical Arab hospitality until they left—and then double down.

Rashid appeared unconcerned and looked at Joseph. "I do believe Christians have an agenda for Syria, but I have nothing but respect for Farid. Especially since I have known his family all these years in Homs." He turned to Farid. "The calls and texts will stop. This is over. I welcome your friendship."

Rashid extended open arms toward the two men seated on

his living room sofa. "We Alawites honor Jesus. We believe Jesus was a great man—a man for the ages! To honor Him is to follow the principles of our Alawite faith." Rashid concluded his acclamation, nodding—a bit too emphatically, Farid thought.

"We have a lot in common, you know. And it's your desire as you've told me to follow Jesus, am I correct?"

"You are correct!" Farid spouted. "Because of that, in fact, I have a gift for you and your family." He reached in his hip pocket and withdrew a rectangular object. "This is a copy of the New Testament. I think one day you may want to get to know Jesus, and if you do, He will be waiting for you in these pages."

Rashid's lip curled as he extended his right hand and pinched the small book between his thumb and forefinger. He raised the New Testament to eye level and studied it as if it were contaminated, then dropped it disdainfully on a nearby bookshelf without saying a word to Farid.

Joseph and Farid exchanged awkward glances and stood slowly from the couch.

Farid forced a smile. "We are thankful to see that your home has not been damaged, Rashid. That's a miracle in Homs, isn't it?" He turned to Um Walid. "Thank you for your hospitality."

The woman glanced nervously at her husband and then walked quickly to the front door.

Joseph said simply, "Good evening to you, Rashid."

Rashid said nothing as the pastors followed their host's wife to the door and stepped outside. Farid and Joseph chose the shortest route back to the Mercedes, picking their way quickly through the wreckage of the Al-Hamidiyah neighborhood.

Halfway to the car, they stopped abruptly at the crack of gunfire, trying to determine the direction from which it came.

Satisfied that it was not between them and the Mercedes, they resumed their pace.

Within sight of the car several minutes later, Joseph asked the question he'd been wondering since leaving Rashid's house. "Farid, do you think he's really done with his threats?"

Farid shook his head. "Not for a moment. His answers were too smooth; he's lying though his teeth."

Farid walked to the passenger side of the car and opened the front door. Before ducking inside, he looked across the roof at Joseph and grinned. "But he does have a copy of the Bible."

The spit of an automatic rifle echoed from a nearby alley.

Farid glanced quickly up and down Hamidiyah Street. "Let's get out of Homs. The sun is going down, and it's going to be a long night in our old hometown."

Farid and Joseph picked up Highway 42 just outside the Ring Road and then turned east on Highway 3 toward Deir ez-Zor. Once on the road beyond Homs, Farid offered a history lesson.

"The new believers in Deir ez-Zor need encouragement. Their city has seen enormous brutality. I'm afraid history is repeating itself there. I'm not sure how many believers are left, but we know of at least seven MBBs[4] who meet at night, and so far, the Islamic State isn't any the wiser.

"Joseph, I believe evil spirits have a vice-grip on Deir ez-Zor. The irony is that the city was built as a refuge for Christians persecuted in the first three centuries. Did you know that's why they built the Mar Elian monastery in the first place? But the whole place has become a scene of torture and persecution.

"And the Armenian holocaust? It will always be associated

with Deir ez-Zor. When the Ottomans banished the Armenians from the empire in the early 1900s, I read that some refugees walked for sixty days before ending up in Deir ez-Zor. And even if they survived the journey, they were murdered shortly afterward.

"It's amazing how few people know that Armenia was the first nation to formally adopt Christianity—in 301, more than a decade before Constantine allowed freedom of religion. So I think killing three-fourths of the Armenian population sixteen hundred years later has been a statement—Muslims killing Christians, pure and simple.

"I've heard that's the reason ISIS gave for choosing Deir ez-Zor as the location to begin their crucifixion campaign. All because the Turks did it to the Armenians here in 1915! This city has generational strongholds, and I think only prayer and fasting will break this cycle of evil."

Joseph hung his head, barely keeping his eyes on the road. "I saw pictures of the sixteen Christian girls from Armenia on the crosses from that year. No doubt they were abused by the Muslim men before they died."

"Yes." Farid's words caught in his throat, his anger building. "Rape is a tool of genocide. So are crucifixions when it comes to murdering Christians." He paused in thought. "When it comes to Armenians, Deir ez-Zor is the Christian version of Auschwitz."

The city once known for the fifteen-hundred-year-old monastery razed by ISIS in August 2015 lay still as Joseph turned onto Bosarayah Street at 4:00 A.M. He parked the Benz on a side street, and the two men scurried behind a row of houses near the Al-Arfi Mosque. They stopped at a darkened home two blocks from the city cemetery. Farid knocked four times on the back door. He startled as the door flew open and a hand beckoned them in.

Stepping inside, they could see that the room was not totally dark. A handful of candles flickered in the dimness. Scanning the room, Farid counted twelve worshippers praying fervently yet lips barely moving. No one acknowledged the newcomers, so Joseph and Farid joined in the quiet prayer.

After an hour and a half, the group prayer ended, and a man who introduced himself as Samir Malouf recounted horrifying news from the previous day. Two teenage girls who would not deny Christ and convert back to Islam had been thrown, hands tied behind their backs, from the roof of a five-story building as their families watched.

As if anchoring the evening news, Malouf segued quickly to his next report. "Then the Islamic State made the announcement that our city will no longer be called Deir ez-Zor. Because 'Deir' means monastery and since that reflects our Christian roots, it has been renamed. We are now in the city of Wilayat ul-Hayr. Ha! Arabic for 'state of goodness.'" The reporter sighed, belying his feelings about the "news."

"There is no good in this city," he continued. "It should be called 'state of evil'!"

Farid broke in. "Samir! Jesus has not forgotten Deir ez-Zor. You are proof of that." He pulled from his hip pocket a small New Testament, much like the one he had given Rashid, flipped to 2 Corinthians, and read to the group:

"'For we do not want you to be unaware, brothers, of the affliction we experienced in Asia. For we were so utterly burdened beyond our strength that we despaired of life itself. Indeed, we felt that we had received the sentence of death. But that was to make us rely not on ourselves but on God who raises the dead. He delivered us from such a deadly peril, and he will deliver us. On him we have set our hope that he will deliver us again."[5]

"Family, not far from here, believers from another generation faced death as well."

The twelve new believers looked up from their Bibles. Farid surveyed each face. The candlelight revealed a resolution that filled him with hope.

"You . . . *We* are each other's new family. And we are not the first to walk this path. As Paul reminds us, believers from another generation—not far from here—faced death as well."

Farid spoke from his heart, stressing how Jesus' love would preserve them and overcome all fear. Thirty minutes into Farid's teaching, one of his listeners' eyes widened, and he nodded toward the wall behind Farid. Farid turned in time to see a stern pair of female eyes at the basement window, peering through a black burqa at the secret meeting. The Islamic State's elite, all-female police unit, the al-Khansa Brigade, was sweeping the neighborhood, looking for young girls ISIS fighters could kidnap—or anyone acting suspiciously un-Muslim. Joseph glanced up from his Bible and saw the shadowy woman. He turned quickly to Farid and then back to the window, but by then, the unwanted visitor was gone.

"Samir, Farid, we must leave—now!" Joseph stood and pointed at the window. "*She* is with the Islamic State. I saw the writing on her hijab. It's almost daylight, so we don't have much time to get out without being seen."

A dozen Bibles slapped shut, and the assembly filed quickly to the door through which Farid and Joseph had entered two hours earlier. One by one, they darted into the alleyway, now visible in the soft early-morning light. Minutes later, Farid and Joseph reunited at the car on Bosarayah Street.

"Farid, should we hide for the day or make a run for it out of Deir ez-Zor before ISIS fighters are out in force?"

"Ha! Joseph, when it rains, it pours! We've got the Islamic State threatening us in this city, and the Alawites threatening us in Homs. This must be what the apostle Paul felt like!" He paused, patting the pants pocket that held his cell phone. "By the way, Rashid couldn't make it through the night before he sent more threats. His texts are sickening. He's sent *five* since we were at his house. He must have been up all night." Farid stopped again. In the growing light, he could see that the street was, for the moment, still deserted.

"Yes, habibi,[6] let's go."

The two men jumped in the Mercedes. Joseph jammed his key into the ignition and turned it to crank the engine. The two men looked at each other in the silence. Joseph's car wouldn't start. It had happened before.

"C'mon, Lord!" He tried again, and the engine responded with more silence.

Farid hopped out of the car, scrambled around the front right fender, and threw open the hood. He jiggled the battery cables and waved to Joseph to try again. As Farid studied the dead engine, a sound behind him made the hairs on his arms prickle. He glanced over his left shoulder. A half dozen blocks away, a white pickup truck, Islamic State flag flapping in the wind, was racing toward them.

Farid spun his hand, encouraging Joseph to keep trying to start the car. As Joseph turned the key a fourth time, the engine blasted to life. Farid slammed the hood closed, darted around the car to his door, and fixed his eyes on the approaching truck as he ducked into the Benz.

Joseph had seen the ISIS vehicle, and as his friend plopped into the front seat, he jammed the gearstick shift into reverse. The car shuddered as aging gears ground into place.

"I've been having trouble getting it into reverse lately," Joseph noted sheepishly.

"It doesn't matter, brother. In a minute this car will be full of bullet holes anyway. Can you outrun the truck?"

"Of course I can, Farid! This is a Mercedes!" Joseph gunned the car into a U-turn, shifted gears, swung south on Bosarayah Street, and accelerated away from their pursuers.

Watching the rearview mirror more than the road ahead, he muttered, "This is going to be close."

Farid flipped open his phone and prayed about whether or not to call Rima. He looked over his shoulder. With its significant head start, the truck was now closing fast. He punched in the number for home.

"Rima, my love! We're in trouble in Deir ez-Zor. There's an Islamic State truck chasing us, and I don't know if we can get away this time." He heard his wife gasp. "I want you to know how much I love you. Please hug and kiss our son, and do me a favor. *If they kill us*, don't even think about coming to get me. My body doesn't matter. It won't be me anymore. I'll be safely inside the gates of heaven." He took a deep breath. "Pray for us, love of my life!"

Rima dropped on her knees, face to the floor. Cell phone still in hand, she stretched her arms in front of her and soaked the carpet with her tears. As Farid said good-bye, she heard the clatter of guns, and the phone went dead.

"Right or left, Farid? Right or left!" They had entered town in the dark with only the car's running lights on, and Joseph couldn't remember how to get to the main road out of the city.

"Turn right! Left would take you to the Euphrates. Look for Highway 4. Hang a right just past the cemetery, and head for Palmyra."

Overflowing with ISIS fighters, the Toyota pickup careened around the corner after the Mercedes. The first shower of bullets from the pursuers had missed widely, but as the truck stabilized on the straight road behind them, Farid watched through the back window as the men in black hoods lowered their weapons again. Joseph rammed the gas pedal to the floor, and by the time he turned toward Palmyra, the truck full of men who likely thought the ancient car would be easy prey was nowhere in sight.

Farid turned to his friend, wide-eyed. "Joseph, your car doesn't go that fast. That was the Lord! There's no way we could outrun those guys. Were there angels behind us or something?"

For an hour, the two best friends, in shock at the attack and their miraculous escape, said nothing, saving words for phone calls to their wives.

The church Farid and Joseph had started in the Assad apartment was having communion when the two pastors arrived home in Tartous late that afternoon. Rima clutched Farid in an embrace that lasted several minutes. The group watched respectfully as Rima cried quietly. Joseph's wife, Tagreed, kissed her husband's face repeatedly as their two little ones clung to his arms. With that morning's near-disastrous conclusion to the trip, their three weeks away had seemed like an eternity.

Rima loosened her grip around her husband's waist. "Farid, Rashid Abbas is sending letters now. I didn't want to tell you more bad news while you were on the road. I threw the letters away, but it frightened me. How did he know where we live? He says he will come to Tartous and kill you if you keep telling Alawites about Jesus."

She pressed her head hard into Farid's chest. "I'm tired of his threats. It's wearing me down. The man is obsessed and has nothing but evil in his soul!"

Farid laid his right hand softly on the back of the young woman's head. "Sometimes I get tired, too, Rima. The past years of unrelenting meetings with the secret police have taken a toll on us." He chuckled. "Remember when one of the questioners said I was the secret police's best customer? How many near misses with death have we had? Too many to count, I'm afraid. And thirty death threats spray-painted on the wall outside our apartment was certainly a new experience for us. I'm sure that was compliments of Rashid Abbas.

"But, Rima, in all of this I have felt God's peace. Enemies of Christ have assaulted us, and I've had to fight to keep my thinking fixed on Jesus. I admit that I sometimes feel like an olive crushed in a press, yet I've learned some truths that will stay with me for the rest of my life—however long or short it may be."

Rima looked up at her husband as he continued.

"Habibti, here are three lessons the Lord has given me: we are victors not victims; the gospel is never in retreat; passivity and fear bring surrender.

"I actually feel sorry for Rashid. His hatred is so acidic he must have trouble sleeping at night."

A new thought occurred to Farid, and he stepped back from

his wife's embrace and spoke to the group assembled in his living room. "Family, join me in praying for Mr. Abbas."

For half an hour, the Assad house church prayed for the Alawite man who hated their shepherd. The prayer gathering of former Alawites represented everything Rashid despised about Farid and his ministry. To him, this scene would be proof that Farid deserved death: converting Alawites is the reason for civil war in Syria—and the hideous Christian agenda.

At the end of the meeting, the new believers hugged one another, many with teary eyes as they left the apartment. Once the door closed behind the last participant, Farid put his arm around Rima and led her to the couch. The two sat quietly, sipped strong coffee left over from the group meeting, and gazed out their seventh-story window toward the Mediterranean Sea. The peace of the calm waters seeped into their hearts.

After several minutes, Farid kissed the top of Rima's head as it rested against his shoulder. "Rima, as difficult as this is, God's work is expanding. It's hard to believe how many people are seeing that Jesus is the only answer to the war and hatred in Syria and the misery it causes in their personal lives. Only Jesus could bring enemies together this way."

He swept his hand toward the room in which the house church had just met. "It's the worship that blows me away. How do former Alawites and Muslims seem to know how to worship Jesus so wholeheartedly so soon after deciding to follow Him? This is an Acts 2 experience, I tell you. Joseph told me that some of the Alawite house church *leaders* are men that he and I have not even met yet. There are fourth-generation believers now leading others."

Farid leaned his head on the back of the couch. "Muslims and Alawites are searching for something in this war. This is about more than hatred toward each other and a civil war. People in both religions have big holes in their hearts that only Jesus can fill. And when He does, look out world! Rima, that's why we have to reach *both* sides of those at war in Syria!

"So many of them are leaving as refugees. We could well be launching a wave of missionaries into the *Western world*. I know that if we *don't* reach them, it will be a wave of terrorists headed there." He pushed gently away from Rima.

"Speaking of terrorists, when I go back to see Rashid, I'd like you to go with me. I'm going to confront him about his threats again, and I think you would like his wife. I'm sure her marriage is a disaster, being stuck with him and his raging anger. You could encourage her."

"When do you plan to go back?" Rima asked, worry in her voice.

Farid sighed and shook his head. "Not tonight, that's for sure. We all need a little time."

Two weeks later, Joseph, Farid, and Rima settled into the forty-year-old car for the ninety-minute ride to Homs.

"I'm sorry to be late." Joseph glanced back at his passengers. "I was actually going to be on time for once, but when I walked out the front door with my family to pray before leaving, we realized that Rashid now has my address too. Someone had stapled threatening notes all over our front door."

Joseph turned south on Highway M1. "Farid, you don't seem a bit concerned about taking your wife to meet the man who wants to kill you." Joseph looked in the rearview mirror at Farid and Rima sitting close, holding hands.

Farid looked up as if staring beyond the roof of the car. "I thank our Father in heaven that He has calmed my heart. I don't feel nervous at all. Rima and I are meant to make this visit together! And, Joseph, thanks for being our chauffeur." He gestured at the back window. "I also like the new paint on the Benz. You've expanded the rainbow."

"Another color looks better than the bullet holes, right? Deir ez-Zor was a close call. Too close." Joseph forced a smile. "Leaving the back side of the car looking like it had just been through target practice would give our Islamic State friends the pleasure of knowing they almost got us. I want God to be glorified—not the enemies of the cross! So I make it a point to erase Satan's footprints as quickly as possible. I learned an important lesson this year: We are not afraid, and we will not be intimidated, will we?"

Joseph glanced at a car entering from the cloverleaf junction.

"Farid, we see miracles every day in Syria. But the works of God in the lives of the new believers are, to me, the most dramatic. They bring me hope just when we need it most. When I think of all the threats we've received . . ." The words caught in his throat. "I get choked up thinking about one particular new believer.

"The threats spray-painted on your front wall intimidated the heck out of most of the new believers. It was a wake-up call to brand-new followers of Jesus that someone actually wanted to kill you because of your faith.

"But then along came Hamdi, the first Alawite believer in over one hundred years. He drove through the night from Alawite Mountain, around the most dangerous checkpoints, got all the way to your place—which was certainly being watched—and painted over every one of the threats! After he left, it looked as if the threats were never there.

"Now, that was a statement!" As Joseph checked the rearview mirror again, Farid saw the tears in his eyes. "The Alawite religious leaders knew that they had lost control for good. Their promises to persecute and kill us didn't faze anyone after Hamdi. Did you know that he even said he flew through the checkpoints with cans of paint on the front seat, as if none of the guards even saw him? Maybe they didn't!"

Joseph raised his right hand and pointed skyward with his index finger. "Hamdi was saying to the religious leaders: 'You cannot intimidate us. If you want to kill Farid and all the other Alawite believers, you better start with me. I was the first one!' He called me right after he finished the paint job and said, 'Joseph, we can't let Satan win this! I just erased the threats.'

"Because of his confidence, I felt the power of God come over me and renew my faith. Ever since then, I've had a new resolve. I absolutely am not afraid anymore. Jesus is with us in this fire!"

As Joseph finished speaking, Farid and Rima looked at each other, tears in their eyes, both thinking of "life since Hamdi." More than four hundred Alawites were now believers.

Farid swallowed the lump in his throat. "Well, Joseph, we are stepping into the fire again tonight—meeting the man who is fanning the flames!"

Hamidiyah Street had not changed in the two weeks since Joseph and Farid first experienced the horror of the city laid waste. On the way into town, they observed in the deepening dusk that the direction of gunfire in Homs seemed random. Orange tracer rounds crisscrossed the skies.

Since a half mile before the traffic circle, they had seen no cars other than burned-out wreckage. Nearing the pile of building where they had parked on their previous venture into Homs, Joseph rolled down his window to listen for activity. As the car crawled forward, lights off, Joseph heard only a distant minaret speaker jubilantly chanting, "Allahu Akbar." The Islamic State was advancing again.

Joseph passed the pile of rubble that marked their earlier parking spot and turned onto Al-Hadhara Street. Eyes flitting from side to side as the car inched up the dark road, Joseph braked in front of a familiar house. He turned off the engine and leaned over the seat back so he, Farid, and Rima could pray a blessing on their meeting with Rashid.

The twenty feet from the curb to the doorstep felt to Farid like a war-zone no-man's land. To his surprise, the front door opened before the trio reached the house.

Um Walid stood in the doorway, smiling. "What an unexpected pleasure to have you visit us, especially on such a dangerous night like this." She looked from the two men to Rima. "Farid, your wife is lovely."

Rashid's wife welcomed them into her living room. Farid saw that Rashid was not in the room. A quick scan also told him that the New Testament he had given Rashid was no longer on the shelf. *Has he thrown it away?* Farid wondered.

While the four exchanged pleasantries, Um Walid beckoned the group to follow her into the kitchen so she could brew some tea. As Farid stepped into the room, his mouth gaped. There it was—the New Testament—*on the kitchen table.* It could mean only one thing: since Um Walid would never touch the book against her husband's will, Rashid must have left it there.

Thirty minutes later, Rashid's wife and her guests sat in the living room, sipping tea. They startled in unison as Rashid burst into the room. He frowned at Farid and nearly shouted, "I've been waiting for you! Is your phone not working? You didn't respond to my calls and SMS messages. Didn't you get them?"

Farid searched for the right words. "I did, Rashid, but . . . well, I've been busy since we saw you a few weeks ago." He stopped, scowling.

"I don't have time anymore for your threats." Farid stood up and faced Rashid. "I'm tired of reading your death wishes for me, Rashid. I come tonight in the name of Jesus, and I want this to stop! If you want to kill me, now's your chance!"

Color drained from Rima's face. She grabbed her husband's arm. "No, Farid!"

Farid pulled away from his wife and walked to the middle of the living room. His knees bent slowly as Farid lowered himself into the execution position. Bowing his head, he spoke again. "Go ahead, Rashid. Get your knife—the one you promised to kill me with. I'm ready to die for Jesus."

Rashid stood motionless, gawking at the spectacle in his living room. The three people still sitting stared at Rashid, too shocked to speak. Slowly Rashid's head turned from Farid to the others, then back to the man kneeling on the floor. Rima gasped quietly and covered her mouth with a hand as Rashid stepped haltingly in Farid's direction until he stood over Farid. A tear rolled down Rima's cheek and dripped to the carpet.

Rashid placed his right hand firmly on Farid's shoulder and slowly dropped to his knees. He leaned forward so he could look Farid in the eye.

"You're asking me to kill you?" Rashid smiled, looked from

Farid to the others, and then back at Farid. "How could I do that . . . to a brother in Christ?"

Rima cried out and began sobbing.

For nearly ten seconds, Farid did not move as he absorbed the words he had just heard. *Yes*, he thought. *Rashid's been reading*. Farid crumpled forward onto the floor, his sobs blending with his wife's. Rashid slid the hand on Farid's shoulder across his old friend's back and bent over him, tears now flowing.

Rashid could only whisper the words. "Please forgive me, my brother."

For several minutes, no one spoke as the group of five wept together. Rashid regained composure first. He stood and pulled Farid to his feet. Rashid extracted a folded piece of paper from the back pocket of his trousers.

"Farid, this is for you." The new believer handed the pastor a letter.

The hand of Rashid Abbas writes this letter.

In the name of the Lord Jesus Christ, whom I now live for, I cancel every threat I have made to Farid Assad. I take them back and lay them at the cross. My hatred for Farid knew no bounds because I thought he was a direct threat to the Alawite religion and to my family. As a result, it was my full intention to end his life.

But something held me back even when I had the chance to carry out my evil deed. I know now that it was the Holy Spirit who restrained me.

To Farid and the many Alawites who now follow Jesus, I ask that you forgive me, and I pray that, after some time, you will receive me as a brother in the faith. Jesus has set me free, and I am free indeed. I apologize to all of you for the fear that my promises to kill you may have instilled in your hearts. Yet, you didn't leave the area, and you prayed for me. I am eternally grateful. Jesus overcame your fear. He overcame mine too.

One night I could feel no peace in my heart. The battle for Homs was at a boiling point. I was reading the Koran and so unsettled. I finally put it aside and I said to it: "I am sorry. You let me down, and your words are empty."

After I put down the Koran, I picked up the Bible that dear Farid gave me. It was 7 p.m. The next time I looked at the clock, the sun was coming up over Homs, and it was 6 a.m. I was falling in love with Jesus. Over the next few days, I soaked myself in the Word of God. I hardly went anywhere. Jesus came to me every night in a dream as well during that holy time. I follow Jesus now. I asked Him to forgive me.

I declare my love for Jesus and I commit to follow my Savior the rest of my life. I also will die for Him if He calls me to that. That's what His faithful do. I knew all about that before I read the Bible. I learned that from Farid.

Please forgive me,
Rashid Abbas

A FINAL WORD FROM FARID

Rashid handed me the letter and asked me to do him a favor: "Put it on your front door, Farid." He wanted it there as a sign of his repentance and as an encouragement to other new believers.

I did put the letter on the front door eventually, but I had to do something else first. A week after our emotional meeting in Homs, I had a surprise for the home group meeting at my house in Tartous.

"Tonight we have a new believer with us," I announced. "He is a little nervous about meeting you, but I know you will greet him with the love of Christ."

Rashid Abbas walked in the front door, and the group sat stunned as he read his letter. When Rashid finished, his new family mobbed him.

Rashid's transformation brings up a few questions I have for you. Is there anyone in your life that you need to reconcile with? Is there anyone that dislikes you even to the point of hatred? If there is, just remember this: Rashid wanted to kill me for five years. But Jesus, who lives in me, gave me the ability to love him anyway. I could not do this humanly speaking. Neither can you.

As followers of Christ, hate is not an option for us. If you have some in your heart, Jesus has a simple message for you: love your enemies and pray for those who persecute you (Matt. 5:44). In the days ahead, I believe we will all need to learn how to live out this well-known verse from the Sermon on the Mount.

As of this writing, Rashid Abbas is alive and well—and still living in Homs. In the midst of the spiritual firestorm there, he leads a house church in his home. Before he took the lead, I discipled and trained him for a year. But let me tell you: the worship in Homs is sweet despite the destruction of the war. Rashid has taken up writing their group's praise music. His are the first hymns ever written specifically for Alawite followers of Jesus. Can you imagine that? The one who wrote death threat notes is now writing life-giving worship songs. I think our Savior is smiling in heaven over that turnaround!

Yes, Jesus is alive and well in Syria. And—oh yes!—our grave-yard is still empty!

3 MARRIED TO AN IMAM

I f anyone leaves our glorious religion," the imam's eyes spit fire as he searched the crowd gathered for Friday prayers, "that person must be erased."

The fifty or so worshippers gathered at the Aleppo, Syria, Grand Mosque nodded mechanically as the Muslim preacher looked from one upturned face to the next.

"We cannot—will not!—compromise on this. It is our duty to Allah. Anyone who exits Islam will exit this world. We will send them straight to judgment. It will be a lesson for all Muslims that we are the faithful who follow Mohammad's teaching and the model of his life.

"Honor killing of a family member is required. Nothing less is sufficient." The imam's nostrils flared, and he raised his index finger. "If my own mother became an infidel, I would kill her that day!

"Why do I speak of this?" He squinted at his listeners. "It is due to a despicable phenomenon these days here in Syria." He shook his head slowly, gazing at his hearers as if personally threatening each one in the audience. "We hear of Muslims from Muslim families becoming followers of the Naz-zz-zarene!" He snarled the word. "But who is this Isa? He is just a prophet—nothing more! Do . . . not . . . be . . . deceived!"

The words echoed across the open space within the mosque, concluding another of Nabil Kassem's Friday sermons—this noontime message merely a recapitulation of last week's and as many weeks prior as faithful attendees could recall. Killing infidels had become Imam Kassem's preferred theme. Yet the one person he most wanted to hear his message had—once again—been missing from his audience. But he would deal with that problem this evening.

Nabil slammed the open palm of his right hand against Noor Kassem's left cheek, sending her reeling into the kitchen table.

"In all of Syria," he shrieked," I doubt there is any imam whose wife is not present at the mosque when her husband speaks—except mine! Where were you?"

Three children—two girls and a boy—scrambled out of the kitchen to the temporary safety of anywhere else in the house. Friday was the most terrifying day of the week at the Kassem house, especially just after Jumu'ah[1] now that Noor Kassem habitually skipped her husband's teaching sessions. Although raised in a committed Muslim home, the woman's passion for her childhood faith withered after she married the fanatical cleric.

Thirty minutes of words and blows later, Nabil's rage ended abruptly. For several seconds, he stared blankly at the woman's bruised eyes, his lips curling slowly into a sneer, then he spit in her face. His final point made, the imam turned and slithered into his bedroom.

Too brokenhearted to cry, Noor let her head droop. At least he didn't beat the children tonight. A measure of Nabil's disdain for women, his teenage daughters were often targets of his fury. Even at the mosque, girls and women feared his surly stares. Nabil could never control his wife completely, so he made every female pay the price.

Noor retreated to her own bedroom, fed up with religion but desperately wanting truth. No matter Nabil's wrath. She would never again submit to Friday prayers and the vile ranting of her monstrous husband.

"I think I will vomit if I have to listen to Nabil spread any more hatred from the mosque. He does this well enough in our home." Noor stirred her tea and stared at the swirling liquid. "Everyone fears that man's obsessive cruelty. Even the most committed followers must think he's insane."

Noor quickly eyed the people sitting at the two nearest café tables, then looked at the woman across the table from her. "Huda, I think he must have an evil spirit."

Noor trusted Huda Sanara with her most intimate secrets. The two middle-aged women shared the common grief of anguished marriages, but Huda, at least, had been spared the physical violence Noor endured.

"Nabil could not possibly be a worse representative for our religion, Huda. His venom drives people away from the mosque. Who wants to endure such rage every week? Syria has enough hate to go around. Our people need hope, and it will not be found at Friday prayers in the Great Mosque." Noor paused briefly, considering whether to voice her next thought, then drew in her breath and looked her best friend in the eye. "I wish I could sneak into a church sometime."

"Noor, what in the world are you saying?" Huda bit on her lip. "You know talking like that could get you killed. Besides, I doubt there are any churches still standing in Aleppo." She leaned back in her chair. "Would you really risk your life by going to a church in broad daylight? Surely, you're teasing me and just trying to get me to react." Huda stared at Noor, her eyes demanding a response.

Noor sat quietly, and then set her stirring spoon on the table. "I honestly would, if it would give me some peace. I actually thought about going to the Armenian 40 Martyrs Cathedral, but then it got bombed into a pile of bricks, so I gave up that idea." She returned her friend's intense look. "Yes, Huda, I don't even care what you think of me. If I could get relief from the pain I'm living in because of that beast, I would do it. In the middle of the day, I absolutely would walk right into a church.

"And if I was seen going there? So much the better! The disgrace for Nabil would be worth it. Think of it: the great imam and his wonderful teaching led his own wife to seek comfort in a church! Ha! That would shame him for a lifetime." Noor made fists and tapped her knuckles together. "Maybe I'll do that. Maybe I will," she added dreamily.

As a new thought entered her mind, her eyes locked onto Huda's. "Would you ever be willing to go with me to a church? Even more than getting back at Nabil, I need rest for my soul. That's what I need, Huda! I long to have peace in my heart for once." Tears formed in her eyes. "I need peace," she whispered.

Huda waited for several seconds before responding. "Noor."

Huda spoke the name softly. "That's where I found peace."

Noor cocked her head, the words registering. "What do you mean?"

"I found peace, Noor, and it wasn't in the mosque. I found it in church."

Noor gaped at her friend, relieved at the freedom she could now feel to share her thoughts but perturbed not to have heard this before now.

"Well, best friend, were you ever going to tell me about this new development in your life?"

Huda grinned. "Not until I knew you were safe, Noor." She whispered, "I couldn't afford to make a mistake with you. After all, your husband is an imam. With one phone call, he could have me killed."

Noor huffed. "Do you think I would—"

"Shhh!" Huda motioned at the people around her. "Not so loud."

Noor continued in a loud whisper. "Did you really think I would turn on my best friend? Seriously, Huda! How could you think so little of me? Is our friendship not worth anything to you?"

Huda patted her own chest.[2] "Noor, this war is turning the best of friends into bitter enemies. It seems that all kinds of horrible things can be done in the name of God nowadays. We're in a religious war, and I think religion is making people do crazy things in Syria. Our country's falling apart, and religion is splitting the seams open.

"Islam has returned to its sorry roots. The brutality is unbelievable." Huda squeezed her eyes shut as if blotting out a memory then looked again at her friend. "Noor, did you hear that ISIS captured a boy and his father not far from here and gave them the ultimatum to become Muslim or die?" She shook her head. "They both refused, so the beasts beheaded the boy in front of his father, and then they . . . I can hardly say it."

Noor closed her eyes. "I'm afraid to ask."

"They played soccer with the boy's head! They were laughing and rolling it on the ground as the father cried. His tears didn't last long, though. He was also dead a few minutes later. And of course they cried 'Allahu Akbar' the whole time."

Huda turned up the palms of her hands. "God is pleased with that? I don't think so. My God has love in His heart."

Noor sat quietly for several seconds before asking the obvious question.

"Huda, are you saying that you have left Islam and become a follower of Jesus?"

Huda Sanara took a deep breath and told her best friend what she dared not tell anyone else.

"Yes! Jesus is my Savior. He is my everything, Noor."

"The Russians are coming!"

The Kassems' front door slammed hard into the living room wall as Nabil burst in, shouting at his family. Noor jumped up from the couch and embraced her two daughters who had been standing in the middle of the room.

"Pack a small bag with what you need," Nabil ordered. "We're going to Lebanon tonight! Bombing will start soon. The evil empire supports President Assad, and they want to make an example of Aleppo. I believe they'll kill us all."

Their son Hussein ran to his room to pack. His sisters began to cry.

Noor mustered calm in front of her girls. "Lebanon? Where will we stay, Nabil?"

"I know it's only fifty miles to Hatay in Turkey, but mobs of people will be heading there. Lebanon is three times as far, but we can stay in a home in Tripoli instead of a refugee camp. I've already called your family, and they've arranged for a house that we can stay in. I think we'll only be there a short time, and besides, I'll take Lebanon over Turkey any day."

He pointed at Noor, feeling smug that he had contacted her family without her knowledge. "But don't get any ideas about staying there for good, Noor. Syria is my home and yours, too. Everyone, move! Now!"

As the Kassem family packed their bags, Russian planes headed for bombing runs over the Baedeen section of Aleppo where the Free Syrian Army awaited with anti-aircraft missiles. The fight would be bitter.

Fifteen minutes after Nabil's announcement, five Kassems scrambled into their aging Isuzu Trooper and raced south toward the Lebanese border. In the backseat, Sabina and Shireen laid their heads on their mother's lap and closed their eyes as the Trooper approached the first checkpoint. Hussein, sitting in front, stared out the side window.

Stroking the heads of her daughters, Noor's thoughts drifted to Huda. She stopped and pulled the cell phone from under her burqa and punched in a text to Huda. Her message found Huda and the Sanara family on Highway M45 heading west toward Turkey. Relieved to know her friend was on her way to safety, she returned to comforting her daughters.

An hour after the text from Noor, Huda and her family approached the Turkish border, unaware that ISIS fighters had just captured a stretch of highway immediately ahead of them and were actively recruiting. Abdullah Sanara braked to a stop behind a line of traffic, and a half dozen cars ahead, Huda could make out the form of a woman sobbing by the side of the road, next to a car that had passed the Sanaras thirty minutes earlier. But she could not see the reason for the woman's grief: ISIS soldiers had pulled her fourteen-year-old son from the car, forced him behind the wheel of a personnel carrier loaded with explosives, and commanded that he drive toward the next checkpoint—one controlled by Syrian government forces. The inconsolable mother knew she would never see her son again.

Abdullah wheeled the car into a U-turn and accelerated back toward Aleppo while Huda covered her face with her hands and prayed out loud, not caring how her Muslim husband would react to her new way of praying.

"Jesus, You promised to never leave me. I believe and trust You. Please stay with us! There is killing all around, but I am not afraid because I am in You, Jesus. I ask for miracles, Lord. Shine your light into this horrible darkness, and show us the path to safety."

Huda opened her eyes, bracing herself for the verbal lashing she would no doubt receive from her husband, but the man said nothing. He glanced sideways at her, back at the road, and then spoke matter-of-factly. "Keep praying, Huda. Only Jesus can help us now!"

Huda's face relaxed into a smile. Abdullah raised his eyebrows and smiled back, playfully.

"Abdullah, you aren't angry that I just prayed to Jesus?"

The man shook his head. "Not at all. I don't know what's

going on with you, but I found your Bible—the one you hid in the closet behind your shoes. I didn't say anything because I just wanted to watch you. I honestly wasn't sure what to do next." He paused, formulating a question. "Are you now a 'Jesus person'? Is that how you say it?"

Joy swelled in Huda's heart. She could hardly believe the words she had just heard.

"That's a good way to say it, Abdullah." She took a deep breath. "And yes, I am a Jesus person now. How do you feel about that? You've heard Nabil's sermons calling us to kill infidels, like I have become. Why haven't you cornered me and made me confess that I've left Islam?"

Four Sanara children gaped, wide-eyed, from the back seat.

"I thought about it, Huda. I really did." Abdullah stared down the road and sighed. "But the changes I saw in you were hard to believe. The loving way you treated the children and me was so amazing that, well . . ." Abdullah blushed almost imperceptibly. "Honestly, I didn't want it to stop."

He gestured with his right hand, then placed it back on the steering wheel. "You're at peace—even while living in Syria! I think you're the only person in Syria who can smile these days. You're so different, Huda. I know it comes from inside."

His voice softened to a whisper. "How could I even think about harming you?"

Huda marveled at the words. Her steely Muslim husband appeared to be near tears.

"When I came into our bedroom one day, you were on your knees, praying. You were praying for me, Huda. Your back was turned, so I just listened. They were the most beautiful words I've ever heard from you."

He turned his head, wonder in his eyes. "Did Jesus teach you how to pray like that?"

Huda nodded but said nothing, still incredulous at the conversation she was having with her husband.

Abdullah shook his head slowly and stared again at the road ahead. "I'm ashamed to think of how I've treated you, Huda—especially when I heard what you said about me in your prayer."

Huda sensed the man's shame and replied softly, "What did I say about you, Abdullah?" Huda inched across the front seat toward her husband, the man who had treated her as a mere possession for years.

"You said that you forgive me and that you still love me."

"I meant every word of it, Abdullah." Huda leaned the rest of the way across the seat and kissed her husband softly and slowly, her lips plucking a tear off of his cheek.

Just after the junction with Highway 60, Abdullah and Huda could see plumes of smoke from Russian bombs along the northwestern outskirts of Aleppo. Not knowing what else to do, they continued driving toward the city. For the first time in years, the couple held hands.

With her free hand, Huda dialed a number on her cell phone.

"Noor, this is Huda. Don't go to Turkey. ISIS has taken over part of the road."

Noor had answered with her speaker on, and Nabil's voice responded. "We're not headed for Turkey. We're going to Lebanon. You and Abdullah need to head to Tripoli! We'll find a place for you there."

For the next hour, Abdullah picked a way around the besieged city, rerouting whenever explosions erupted in the path forward. Bombs lit the evening sky like lightning. Finally, Abdullah turned south on the Aleppo-Damascus Highway. Somewhere ahead of them, he knew, the imam and his wife were speeding along the road known since the war began as the Highway Through Hell.

As they approached Hama, burned-out vehicles marked the spot of a recent firefight. Wondering what his friend Nabil might do if he knew of Huda's conversion, Abdullah turned to his wife. "Huda, I think it's time for you to pray again."

Abdullah pulled a nearly full pack of cigarettes from his shirt pocket, tapped the box, and placed a cigarette between his lips. As he lit the cigarette and cracked open his window to let the smoke out, automatic gunfire clattered nearby. Behind him, the children winced and dropped to the floor. Huda prayed all the way to the Lebanese border while Abdullah smoked the rest of his cigarettes.

A week later, two best friends relived their miraculous escapes from Syria.

"Noor, when the shooting started on the road between Hama and Homs, I felt sure we were dead. Something would get us—stray bullets, a rocket attack, or maybe ISIS stopping every car and shooting the people inside. But I prayed and remembered Jesus' words: 'Come to Me, all of you who are weary and burdened, and I will give you rest.'

"I kept repeating the verse from Matthew, and it calmed the children. Even Abdullah became noticeably less tense."

"Wait a minute!" Noor cut her off. "You said a verse from the Bible out loud in front of Abdullah, and he didn't scream at you or hit you?"

"No, he didn't, Noor. Things are changing with Abdullah. He's opening up to Jesus.

"And, Noor, I think things are about to change for you. Would you like to go to a Bible study with me tomorrow? It's not so dangerous here in Lebanon."

The next morning, Miriam Basara beamed as she walked into the room of a church in downtown Tripoli. Twelve women in hijabs sat in a circle of chairs. Miriam tried not to feel self-conscious that she was the only one not wearing a hijab. Two of the women sat especially close to each other.

"I can't lie to you, Huda." Noor spoke quietly. "I'm nervous about being here. But when she walked into the room, it felt like the whole place lit up."

"That's Miriam for you. Everyone feels her warmth and love. Not only that, she's one of the funniest people I've ever met." Huda patted Noor's knee. "Relax. Don't be frightened. You'll love reading the Bible. Trust me."

The two-hour meeting passed quickly, and after the other women left, Huda and Noor remained, still sipping the tea served at the conclusion of the Bible study. For years, the two friends had met for tea at least once a week, but this time, complaining about their husbands wasn't on the agenda.

"There is something about Miriam." Noor searched for words. "I want to live like her. I want to pray like her. I want to . . ."

"Follow Jesus?" Huda finished the sentence for Noor.

"I . . . think so." Huda understood Noor's tentative answer.

"Like I told you last night, my dear sweet Noor, wanting that—doing that!—is not so dangerous here in Lebanon . . . But it is extremely dangerous in your house. After all, what's the hot button that sends Nabil into that face-contorting rage of his? Anything to do with Muslims leaving Islam, right? Your following Jesus would be a travesty for him. You would pay for it dearly, and I'm worried for you, Noor.

"On the other hand," Huda wagged her head, "look at how protected I've been since I said yes to Jesus. I'm not sure if it's Jesus Himself or if He's sending heavenly armies, but somehow I have not been in any danger since I decided to follow Him.

"But for you, Noor, it could be a completely different story. Nabil is terrifying, and I'm concerned for you—and the children.

"My advice is that you pray and fast for a week before you make the most important decision of your life. I honestly think Nabil will try to kill you once he finds out that you've given your life to Jesus. It would be the only way for him to save face as an imam. He's preached about honor killings for years."

Noor nodded and blinked back tears as she stared at the floor.

"Noor, I will pray, and you know what? I'm going to fast this week with you."

Huda slid an arm around her friend, and both cried quietly together.

After several minutes, Noor sat straight and looked at her best friend's soft, tear-streaked cheeks. "Huda, if I fast for the week, can we still have tea?"

Huda grinned. "Yes. Yes, we can, my precious friend. I think we should meet every day, in fact. I would give you a Bible, but I'm afraid if Nabil found it, he might kill you before the week of praying is over. So instead, I'll tell you a story from the Bible— over tea, of course—every time we get together. That will give you something to hang on to as you pray."

White skirting on the oversized shade umbrellas at Tripoli's Sense Café flapped in a gentle breeze. The patter merged with the rustle of air moving through a vibrant green hedge surrounding the patio. A sense of well-being embraced the trendy coffee shop as Huda and Noor each stirred a cup of tea for their first meeting of the self-imposed week of fasting.

"Huda," Noor pointed toward the service counter just inside the door of the café, "those desserts are killing me. Maybe this wasn't such a good place to meet while we're fasting. And . . . you said we would pray each day, but how can we do that?" Noor asked, her face serious.

"It's a trick Miriam showed me. She pointed out that prayer is just a conversation with God, and when you follow Jesus, He opens up a direct line of access to the Father in heaven. So . . . I don't have to fold my hands or bow my head. I can simply talk, and Jesus hears.

"It works because, before we confess Jesus as Savior, our sins block us from God. But Jesus took our sins to the cross, and once we repent, He removes them. Then we are clean and can go to God anytime, anywhere. So let me show you how I pray in a situation like this, in order not to attract listening ears."

Huda continued looking at her friend as she spoke, "Dear Jesus . . ." To an observer, it would have looked as if she were simply conversing with the other woman at the table.

At 1:00 in the afternoon seven days later, Noor and Huda sat in the living room of Miriam's house. The week of prayer and fasting had been better than Noor could have dared to hope.

Consumed with getting a job, Nabil spent little time at home and barely noticed his wife or children when he was there.

"I'm ready," Noor began. "I really needed this week to prepare my heart, but I've fallen in love with Jesus. My feelings are reinforced every time I hear Huda pray or tell me a story from the Bible.

"I know this message about Jesus is the truth." She looked soberly at each of her friends. "I'm ready to follow Jesus, and I expect that Nabil will kill me . . . but I don't care about that. Jesus gave up everything for me, and I'm ready to do the same for Him. I've already started to feel peace in my heart, ever since I decided in my own mind that this is what I should do."

Huda and Miriam hugged Noor, and Huda led her friend in a prayer of commitment. After the three women opened their eyes, Noor spoke first.

"I feel so free! For the first time ever, joy has overrun my heart. This is what I've wanted to feel my whole life. Thank you, both of you!" She squeezed her eyes shut and patted her chest. "And thank You, Jesus!"

Miriam placed her hand on the arm of her new sister in Christ. "Noor, your journey begins today. You need to be strong for it." She reached in her purse. "Here's a Bible for you. I recommend that you begin reading in John. Nabil will probably suspect something is up because he's going to see a transformation in you. I have little doubt that he will soon find out you are in love with Jesus. So be wise with this book. He may search the house for it. As long as you have this Bible, though, it will guide you every day."

At the thought of Nabil, Miriam bit her lip before continuing. "If Nabil gets suspicious, have you thought about what to tell him?"

Noor shook her head. "I haven't figured that out. But I suppose that since prayer is an ongoing conversation with God, He and I are in for a long visit today. Jesus will show me what to do . . . Won't He?"

"He will!" Miriam and Huda answered in unison.

As Noor left Miriam and Huda that afternoon, the urgency of her need for a plan about Nabil struck her. Friday prayers were less than twenty-four hours away.

At 11:30 the next morning, Noor watched from the kitchen door as Nabil stood at the counter, stirring a cup of coffee. Leaving the children behind in the living room, she walked quietly toward her husband and stopped an arm's length from him. As he looked up from his coffee, Noor spoke softly.

"Nabil." She glanced at the floor and then at her husband. "I'm not going to the mosque with you today. I'm staying here so I can read my Bible."

For no more than a second, his eyes locked onto her face, then flared as his right fist hammered her jaw. His blinding punch threw the woman to the floor. Noor wrapped her arms around her head to shield her face from follow-up blows as Nabil kicked her body until she went limp.

Having heard their mother's fall, all three children ran into the kitchen and tried to pull their father away from Noor. Nabil grabbed for the two girls, but they squirmed away. He chased his daughters into their bedroom, scrambling to remove his size-11 shoe for their beating, while Hussein scuttled out the front door and ran toward the mosque down the street. Noor did nothing to intervene. It would be an hour before she regained consciousness.

The next day, Huda, Noor, and Miriam huddled in Miriam's living room.

"You didn't waste any time telling Nabil!" Huda studied the purple swelling on Noor's left jawbone. She thought her friend looked like a mixed martial arts fighter who had lost badly.

"I decided to get it out in the open with Nabil right away. But I'm not backing down from my commitment to Jesus. Nabil may think he wins by killing me, but I am not afraid. Nabil told me that I have lost all three children and that he will throw me out of the house. He cannot really do this, though.

"My family owns the house we live in, but I think that's the only thing holding him back."

Noor noticed the relief on Miriam's face.

"Our house is my parents' vacation home, so if Nabil did away with me, he'd be out on the streets. And there's one thing he doesn't even know yet but will be shocked to find out: my parents have put the house in my name."

Noor, Huda, and Miriam met regularly after that, and although the beatings from Nabil were only sporadic, the other two women saw in Noor's face the deep pain she lived with in her home. Nabil could not throw Noor out of her own house, so he was stuck with no place to go. The imam became a caged animal, and after six months, the women sensed that something had to give.

"Nabil made an announcement to me and the children yesterday. He said that if I'm baptized, then he will kill me. He's made a vow to do this."

"Why do you think Nabil would hinge everything on baptism?" Miriam was concerned. "Could it be that he knows one is scheduled for next Sunday afternoon? Noor, I don't know if you were thinking of it, but now is not the time. Since we baptize people every few months, you can do that later. Let this new threat of Nabil's blow over. All of the new believers are concerned for you, and I'm afraid Nabil must know something."

Behind padlocked church doors the next Sunday afternoon, twenty-six former Muslims lined up for baptism, Huda among them. She reviewed in her mind the Bible verse she would share and glowed thinking of the miracle that Abdullah was standing in line behind her.

As Pastor Jamal stood to begin the baptismal service, his eyes riveted on a latecomer at the back of the church. The congregation turned in the direction of their pastor's gaze, and the room erupted in applause. Noor Kassem had joined the line smiling and ready to be baptized.

A WORD FROM NOOR

So why am I still alive? It is only through the protection of God. Nabil promised to kill me if I was baptized. But Jesus called me to baptism, and I did it joyfully for my Savior. I truly figured my life with Jesus on this earth would be short. But He still stands with me here.

Sabina and Shireen are following Jesus too! The horrible beatings from their father did not stop them from running into the arms of their Savior. With Hussein, it took some time. He did not want to disgrace his father, but the call of God on his life was strong. One day he found his sisters and me praying and knelt so quietly beside us that, at first, we didn't even know he was there. It startled us when he spoke, but his words brought such a rush of joy to our hearts!

He said, "Jesus, I do love You too. Please forgive me. And please forgive my father and open his heart that is so hard."

Nabil, though, rages on. Since I still own the home, I told Nabil he could have a room on the other side of the house if he leaves us alone. Many friends told me that was not smart, but Nabil abides by the agreement. He doesn't have anywhere else to go.

Do you have a family member with a stubborn heart? If so, please don't give up on him or her. Do you have a family member you need to forgive? Pray without ceasing, like Paul says. We pray for Nabil every day. At first, I could tell he hated hearing us pray for him, but now I think he likes to listen just around the corner, out of sight.

Because of us, Nabil is learning about Jesus. We make it a point to read the Bible out loud, and since our home is small, he can't help but hear us.

I believe the Savior's love will reach my husband's heart someday. Jesus has given me the grace to forgive Nabil for all the beatings, and he sees it in me. Nabil had never known forgiveness until now. It was not easy for me, of course, but everyone who follows Jesus must learn to forgive—especially someone who is married to an imam.

4 THE MUSLIM WOMAN AT THE WELL

"G et out of my house and never come back!"

Sunni Halabi stood before her husband, guilty as charged. In the Muslim man's eyes, the woman's transgression was worse than mere immorality. She might as well have been a whore.

The marriage was over as soon as Mustafa proclaimed, "I divorce you" three times. No amount of explaining would change his mind. If Sunni could not bear him a child, she would no longer be his wife.

"Mustafa!" Sunni stood next to the kitchen table where the two of them had been finishing dinner when Mustafa exploded. "We haven't even been married three years yet. I know the most important thing in the world for you is to have a child, and especially a boy to carry on the family name. But you know how willing I am to keep trying. I've already had two miscarriages. That's not uncommon. It often happens before a woman gets pregnant and stays pregnant. Please give me more time."

Even as she fought to stay with Mustafa, Sunni merely supposed staying married was better than not. She certainly didn't love the man. Her parents had arranged the marriage to Mustafa. On her own, she would not have chosen him in a million years.

The two of them couldn't have been more different. Sunni smiled at everyone; Mustafa didn't know the meaning of the word. Sunni never met a stranger, but Mustafa's manner made sure everyone remained a stranger to him. And no matter whom he talked to, Mustafa's words sounded more like a growl than actual Arabic.

Still, she didn't want to be sent "to the street" because she had no idea where to go. Her family would bear the shame a divorce would bring on them, and here in Lebanon, it seemed as if bad news traveled at the speed of light. The sideways glances would begin as soon as the last "I divorce you" left Mustafa's lips.

Tripoli might offer her some cover. In the city, scrutiny was not quite as intense as in her family's village. But even so, her parents would chafe under the insults from relatives and neighbors.

Mustafa slammed his fist on the table, catapulting a fork onto the floor, then stood up and grabbed Sunni by the back of her burqa, hauled her to the open back door, and shoved her across the threshold so hard that she nearly fell on the concrete patio. Mustafa slammed the door shut, and Sunni heard the deadbolt click into place. She was now a twenty-three-year-old divorced Muslim woman.

Sunni turned from the house and walked slowly to the back alley, gathering her thoughts. By the time she reached the road, though, she held her chin up and headed briskly toward the bus station near Tell Square.

How did I manage to stay with Mustafa this long anyway? she asked herself.

Within fifteen minutes, she was nearly skipping along the road. Freedom! She loved the thought and stopped to drink in the moment. Her eyes drifted up the beige stonework of the

Al-Tell Clock Tower, evening lights elongating the edifice, until her gaze locked onto the century-old clock. A new thought formed in her mind: *Time to wake up from my nightmare.*

Standing just outside the Center of Tripoli Bus Station a few minutes later, her spirit still soared at the thought of never returning to Mustafa. She could think of only one thing that would dampen the emotions of the moment and sighed as she pulled the cell phone from under her burqa and dialed her mother's number.

"The torture is over, Ami."[1] Sunni cast the best spin she could think of on the news her mother was bound to hate. "Mustafa has divorced me. He cannot take another day if his wife is unable to bear children. And I cannot take another day if my husband won't love me."

"Marriage is torture, my dear Sunni. That's how it is." Her mother's cold response felt like a kick in the stomach.

"How can you say that, Ami? You and Baba have a good life together."

"We do, I suppose. But I gave up all my dreams to serve him. Yet I do not think he gave up anything for me. I stuck it out, Sunni, and so should you."

"Are you forgetting something, Ami? Mustafa divorced me. It's over. There's nothing for me to do. I can't try any harder to get pregnant. You would think even he would agree that every night is enough."

The woman on the phone ignored her daughter's argument. "Yes, there is something you can do. You can turn around and go back to him. If you plead, he will take you back. Eventually you will have a baby. Just keep trying. After all, don't I deserve a grandchild?"

Sunni resisted the temptation to hang up on her mother and instead challenged her. "So that's what this is about? You think if I don't cower back to Mustafa, you'll never have a grandchild? Do you really want your daughter to beg like a street woman?" Sunni felt her face flush with anger, and she jabbed the "off" button of her phone.

The bus for Bazbina village would be running another day—if she ever decided to go home—and she stepped away from the bus station entrance to head back up the street. She knew of a friend who would take her in.

The phone conversation with her mom would have been just the prelude. Once home, her mother would lecture some more, then her father's speech might turn into a beating. But worst of all would be Zakaria. Although her brother was only three years older, he had treated Sunni with contempt far beyond his years for as long as she could remember. Leaving his tirades behind had been the best thing about marrying Mustafa.

Amina placed a cup of tea on the small rectangular table between the two patio chairs. Street noises drifted up from below, just distant enough to make Sunni feel safe from the world on the third-floor balcony of her best friend's apartment.

"Can you believe my own mother wants me to stay in my absurd marriage? I can't believe all she cares about is that I have children so she can have grandchildren. How sad is my life? All I've ever wanted to be was a wife whose husband really loves her."

Sunni picked up her teacup and sipped the contents. "But this is an illusion, right?" She looked at her friend through the steam rising from her mug. "Am I hoping for the impossible?"

Amina, a single career woman, frowned. "When I lived in Bazbina, my family was obsessed with marrying me off too! I could have been so-ooo-ooo happy—that is, if I didn't mind being married to someone old enough to be my father! Now that I'm on my own, all I have to do is fight off a few fat old men now and then—okay, maybe every other day!"

The two women giggled.

"My advice to you, my dear Sunni, is to not go back to your family. Avoid them, because you know what? I guarantee that they are already looking for someone to take their daughter off their hands again. You made only one phone call, but they probably have your next husband picked out for you already. They have to, Sunni. You are a curse now—a barren, divorced woman in a Muslim family."

Sunni smirked and bobbed her head playfully, trying to make light of her situation, but Amina's words rang true. "The last thing I ever want is to have my mother and father pick out another husband for me. I don't care if I'm single for the rest of my life. I let them 'arrange' things for me before, and look where it got me."

But Sunni's resolve was short-lived. Her mother pleaded with her to come home, and after six weeks of sleeping on Amina's couch, Sunni relented. Going home was as bad a decision as she had feared the first afternoon on Amina's balcony, and two years later, Sunni was eighteen months into a worse marriage than hers with Mustafa.

Using all the traditional rationale and manipulation, her parents had coerced her into marrying a man of their choice "for her protection." After all, as a divorced woman she would be safer with a husband and not seen as fair game by the men who were drawn to her beauty and enchanting personality.

But one morning, Sunni studied herself in the bathroom mirror. *Am I dreaming, or did I really fall for my mother's schemes again? Ghassan is a creep! I can't believe I'm stuck with such a detestable man. How can I be married to someone twice my age? I must be the biggest fool in the world.*

Twenty-five years older than Sunni, Ghassan Hariri's favorite thing about Sunni was the bragging rights the superb young wife provided in his circle of friends. The second night of their marriage, he spent until well after midnight smoking the nargila at a local coffee shop and telling his friends about the first night of their marriage. Ghassan explained that his previous wife had been a mistake that Sunni would make up for. She would bring him happiness for years to come—and several children too. During prenuptial negotiations, Sunni's parents had neglected to mention their daughter's difficulty in getting—and staying—pregnant.

Seven nights after the wedding, the beatings had begun. The obsessive-compulsive Ghassan demanded perfection in all things. If he found so much as a dish out of place in the kitchen cabinets, Sunni paid the price in beaten flesh. Dinner became the most stressful time as he reviewed the day and gave Sunni her grade. Invariably, she didn't cut it and needed improvement in multiple areas. So in front of the bathroom mirror that day, she decided it was time to see Amina again.

"I have thrown my life away once more. How could I have been talked into this dreadful existence? My mother and father may be masters of manipulation, but my brain also must have ceased to function while they picked out Ghassan. First I was rejected for being a barren wife, and now I'm in a forced second marriage worse than before. At least Mustafa never beat me, even though I was pretty sure he hated me. I just failed as the incubator for the children he wanted."

Amina grabbed Sunni's hand and looked her friend in the eye. "You can't let your parents run your life anymore! Leave Ghassan and don't look back. He's a heartless old man who doesn't deserve you. Sunni, you can hide at my apartment as long as you need to." Amina slid her hand gently up her friend's arm. "How did you get this bruise? Did Ghassan do it?"

Sunni's head drooped. "It makes me sick even to look at his hideous face. I think Ghassan must have some sort of evil power over me. I know the horrible things he says aren't true, but I always accept them and try to do better the next day. But then he beats me again. His complaints are just the excuse he needs to satisfy his violent urges. Then he takes me to the bedroom." She shook her head. "What a life I have."

Both women sat quietly for several seconds. Then Sunni sighed. "Should I have stayed with Mustafa?"

"Are you serious, Sunni? You shouldn't have married either one of them to begin with. You definitely shouldn't stay another day with this present monster. Don't go back. Please, Sunni. Ghassan will be home soon, and tonight will be no different from all the others. You're safe with me. I insist you stay." As if to emphasize her point, Amina got up from her chair in the small kitchen, stepped over to the stove, and began preparing tea.

With her back to Sunni, she continued. "Your parents will forgive you someday. I think even they will come to their senses. Mine haven't yet, but I refuse to have them run my life anymore. Seeing your failed marriages, though, should help your parents. But no matter what, it's time for you to take charge of your life, Sunni."

At twenty-five, Sunni procured her second divorce, but this time, she did the initiating, reports from Ghassan notwithstanding. Too self-important to admit failure, he announced to his family that he had sent Sunni away, citing her multiple shortcomings and vowing to spread the news throughout Tripoli that Sunni had mental problems. Because she had failed as a wife, he would move on to someone better.

But Sunni moved on even more quickly. Elated once again to be free from a toxic marriage, she ignored the barrage of phone calls from her parents. Instead of talking with them, she texted every few days to say she was busy with her new job.

Eight months into her new life, she and Amina shared a late-evening dinner on Amina's balcony and reflected on the changes.

"Thank you for getting me the job at the Four Seasons, Amina. You were a true friend to stick your neck out for a newbie like me. I don't have any hotel experience, but you know I'm working hard to prove I can handle it." She let out a breath. "This is a new world for me, Amina. I can't believe I'm working, bringing in my own money, and not dependent on a husband for survival."

She paused, debating how to say what was on her mind. "Did you know that our religion is changing?"

Amina raised one eyebrow and cocked her head toward Sunni.

"I'm meeting Muslims who still practice Islam but somehow manage to live in the reality of the twenty-first century."

Amina did not comment. She wondered where this was leading.

"I have hope again. I don't really want to get married anytime soon, but have I ever met some real lookers!"

"Any in particular?" Amina responded, caution in her voice.

"Well, there's a man from Jordan—a really successful businessman—and he should be in a magazine. He's gorgeous!"

Sunni blushed and shoveled the rest of the hummus from her plate into her mouth. Amina smiled at the changes in her friend.

"It's like I've told you all along, Sunni. We . . ." she pointed back and forth between the two of them, "are strong women who are not dependent on men to bring us happiness. The only thing men have brought you so far is misery. But look at you now! You have a career, and you're going places." She winked playfully at her friend. "And I hear there's an opening at the hotel in Jordan on the Dead Sea. What would you think about a transfer?"

Sunni stopped guzzling tea and looked up from her cup, eyes wide. "Do you think I could . . . do you think they would take me?"

"They might. But first . . ." Amina raised her right index finger authoritatively. "You need to cool it with noticing great-looking guys. Work on your career, and if you want to get married later—maybe in your thirties—then go for it." Amina cocked her head, a you-better-listen-to-me expression on her face. Sunni, grateful for her friend's concern and good advice, just smiled.

Although Sunni understood the value of Amina's career development talk, her heart pushed toward other goals. She was in search of love and just knew she would someday meet her true love at the front desk of the Four Seasons Hotel. Abounding in handsome and successful guests, it seemed the perfect place to screen a potential husband. Many patrons came from places other than Lebanon, and that, too, was certainly fine with Sunni.

Two weeks later, the pair of friends again sipped evening tea on Amina's balcony.

"Amina, is the job still open in Jordan?"

"No. I'm afraid not, Sunni, but why do you ask?" Amina suspected a motive other than career advancement.

Sunni raised her eyebrows. "I met the most amazing man from Amman. Actually, he's the one I already told you about. He's back from Jordan this month for the second time; he's single and never been married. And he started flirting with me as soon as he checked in. He came up with so many excuses to ask for things at the front desk that it got embarrassing. I can tell he likes me, and right now he's planning to stay for a month. He says he's starting a business that will even help Syrian refugees. Now that's the kind of man I could marry. And it doesn't hurt that he's a perfect gentleman."

Amina stroked her chin and shook her head. "Do you really want to go down this road? You're twenty-six years old, and men have been a disaster for you. Do you really think the third time's the charm? And what would your parents think without having any say in your marriage? They would probably disown you."

"I'm afraid it's too late to worry about that, Amina. They might as well have disowned me already. I can hardly bear my mother's guilt trips about the two failed marriages, but that would change if I married Maged and gave her lots of grandchildren. In her eyes, that would make up for my failures. Mustafa and Ghassan would be forgotten, and she'd be proud of me once again."

"I don't feel good about this, Sunni. Please go slow."

"Slow" lasted two months. Her parents' smiles at Sunni and Maged's wedding ceremony masked their displeasure at not being consulted on the choice of their daughter's third husband, but it was hard even for them to feel too badly about a wealthy businessman from Amman who looked like a cover model for

GQ magazine. Sunni had finally made it, and her parents were, at the very least, relieved.

Wildly in love with her husband of six months and with the lifestyle he provided, Sunni saw Maged as the man she had dreamed of since she was a young girl. He even retained a hint of mystery that added to the magnetism of her magic man. Part of it, she knew, was simply the unheard-of freedom he gave her. Although they needed none of her income, he had even moved with her to a luxury apartment in Tripoli so she could continue working at the Four Seasons Hotel. Yet, as good as it all seemed, there were times she wished to know more about the mysterious source of their never-ending stream of wealth. Lounging close to her husband and lover on their leather couch just after breakfast one morning, it seemed the perfect time to bring up the subject again.

"Maged, I know you like treating me lavishly, but I'm really curious about where it all comes from. What exactly do you do for a living? You've talked about selling property, and I assume you mean real estate. But your business deals in Jordan and Lebanon bring us so much money so quickly I wonder what kind of real estate. Do you buy and sell apartment buildings?"

As Maged set aside his *Daily Star* newspaper, Sunni saw the titillating, mysterious flash in the man's eyes even before he replied.

"We're having a guest for dinner this evening, Sunni. He'll be spending the night with us, so can you have the guest room ready? You're going to like him. He's met you at the hotel already."

"Is he a business client? Staying here is fine if that's what you want, but I'm curious about why he wouldn't stay at the Four Seasons."

"Well, Sunni, he's a new client, and he really wants to stay with us."

Sunni welcomed Jamal Dijani at their front door just past 4:00 that afternoon. She did, in fact, recognize the fortysomething man with wisps of gray in his temples, from checking him in at the Four Seasons, but she had never noticed his probing eyes as she did this evening. His looks made her uncomfortable—and so did the package tucked under his right arm. After settling him in the living room, she retreated to the kitchen to make fresh coffee. Passing Maged at the door to the kitchen, she whispered her concern.

"Maged, did you know that Mr. Dijani brought alcohol with him?"

"Yes." Maged pursed his lips, feigning concern. "He's a secular Muslim, but that's okay. I meet many like him in business and simply have to accommodate them. I don't drink, of course, but to make him feel at home, I will join him tonight." He touched his wife's shoulder and then turned to greet their visitor.

After dinner and three rounds of whiskey, Dijani winked at Maged and announced he was ready for bed. Relieved that the drinking party had ended, Sunni stood from her seat at the dining room table and smiled politely at the couple's guest. "Thank you for staying with us tonight, Mr. Dijani. I'll see you in the morning." Sunni nodded, picked up three empty glasses, and turned toward the kitchen.

Maged stood quickly and reached for Sunni's arm. She stopped as he applied gentle pressure to turn her toward the two men. "Actually, Sunni, you don't need to bother with the dishes just now. You'll be seeing Mr. Dijani before tomorrow. In fact, you will be sleeping with him tonight."

Sunni glanced at the middle-aged guest, then quickly back at her husband, not comprehending what he had just said. She puzzled over the strangely gentle expression on his face and the instructive look in his eyes. "You will do this," he seemed to be saying. She stared at her husband for thirty seconds. The silence did not seem awkward to the two men as the meaning of this gradually dawned on the woman.

Eyes on Maged's wife, Dijani slid his chair back from the table and stood up. He swayed for several seconds, the effects of too much whiskey evident, then stumbled in the direction of the guestroom. Sunni watched him cross through the living room, then looked blankly at Maged. Her husband said nothing, so she placed the glasses she had intended to wash back on the table and followed Mr. Dijani to the bedroom. Tears trickled down her cheeks as Dijani closed the door behind them.

Amina stared, wide-eyed, across her kitchen table at her best friend.

"I knew Maged was too good to be true! The property he's selling is women! Sex-trafficking, Sunni! Your husband is a pimp!" She covered her mouth with a hand, and then continued. "Ya ilahi,[2] he even sold you. Did you sleep with the man?"

Sunni shook her head. "I didn't have to. Mr. Dijani must've been drinking before he came over, and the whiskey after dinner did him in. I promised to freshen up in the guest bathroom, and while I was stalling, he fell asleep. When I opened the door, he was sprawled on the bed, snoring. Fortunately, he hadn't even taken his clothes off before passing out. So I slipped out of the room and slept on the couch."

Sunni leaned back in her chair and looked at the ceiling. "Amina, am I a magnet for sick men? Is that my lot in life? How can I stay with Maged? I couldn't even look at him this morning." Sunni wept as she thought of the dream-shattering night.

"That is one of the lowest things I've ever heard of a husband doing to his wife. Prostituting you while he stayed in the same house! Are you kidding me? Sunni, you are my best friend, and I hate to break it to you, but Maged doesn't love you. You're just cover for him, so he can look like a respectable businessman—which he obviously is not!"

Amina reached across the table and placed a hand on Sunni's left forearm. "Don't go back. I don't care whether this is your third or tenth divorce. Leave him now. What he did to you was criminal."

Sunni stayed with Amina and heard nothing further from Maged. Less than a week after the incident with Mr. Dijani, Sunni heard from a neighbor that her husband had moved out of their apartment. Marriage number three was over.

Marriage number four lasted just over twenty-four hours. Zakaria could not believe his sister had so disgraced the family as to have three failed marriages and threatened their parents that he would get legal control of Sunni and make her stay married if they did not. The trio forced Sunni into marrying another man from Bazbina, who now lived in Tripoli.

But Sunni was Hosni's second wife, and on their first day

together, he explained the new arrangement to Sunni: she would be a servant to Hosni and his first wife. Sunni left Hosni and wife number one in the middle of the second night.

For the two months that followed, Sunni spiraled deeper into depression. She could no longer go home to her parents and had tired of running to Amina after the latest disaster of a marriage, but with nowhere else to go, she ended up once again at Amina's apartment.

"How come the happiest days of my life are always when I get divorced? That's just not right, Amina. I think I need some pretty serious counseling. I'm really messed up."

The two friends talked late into the night yet came to no new conclusions on what Sunni should do next except to see a "new friend" of Amina's. The following day, Sunni joined the charming Christian woman at a local coffee shop and found herself uncharacteristically open within their first few minutes together.

Miriam Basara smiled. "We're *all* messed up, Sunni. That's the human condition."

The words "human condition" sounded strange yet meaningful to Sunni.

"But, Sunni, how did you hear that I do counseling?"

"Amina told me that you help all women whether they're Muslim or Christian, and I think that's wonderful. But I'm sure you've never met anyone as dysfunctional as me. My life is like a bad movie that won't end. I'm just not sure what to do anymore." She paused and studied the other woman's face. "Miriam, how can you smile so kindly when I am baring my heart—screwups and all—to you?"

"Sunni, don't let my expression make you think I'm not

taking seriously your every word. I'm smiling because I know Someone who will help you—guaranteed. I've heard other stories like yours. In fact, there's a group of 'messed up' people that gets together tomorrow, and I'd love for you to come visit. Because of the refugee crisis in Syria, we have lots of new women there. It's a Bible study Amina has been coming to for a few weeks and so have Noor and Huda from Syria. I think she's mentioned them to you."

Sunni studied Miriam for several more seconds and then surprised Miriam with a simple response. "I'll be there."

As Sunni headed back toward Amina's apartment after meeting with Miriam, a familiar number showed up on her cell phone. She hesitated before answering. "Zakaria, my dear older brother who conspired with our parents to push me into a vile marriage with Hosni, I'm not sure I ever want to speak to you again. So why am I talking to you right now? I really don't know." Sunni doubted that she could ever forgive her arrogant and domineering brother, but few things could have surprised her as much as Zakaria's first words back to her.

"Sunni, I want to apologize to you. I have treated you badly and judged you unfairly for your divorces. You have never done anything to hurt me, but I know I've been hurting you for years. Can I please see you so I can apologize in person?"

Sunni waited several seconds before asking what seemed like the obvious question.

"So," she huffed, "have Mother and Father sent you to kidnap me in order to hand me off to yet another husband they've chosen?"

"No, Sunni. I understand why you would wonder such a thing, but that's not it at all—I promise you. I truly want to meet with you to ask forgiveness. It's on my head."[3] Sunni agreed to meet him for dinner—the first time her brother had ever offered to pay for a meal together.

Zakaria launched the conversation with a question that stunned his sister: "Sunni, do you think we're in the wrong religion? I mean, look at everything happening around us. Muslims are killing Muslims in the name of Allah, and it seems like the Middle East is drowning in a sea of hatred.

"I know you've been searching for love, and so far marriage hasn't been the answer. It makes me wonder if there's more."

Through most of the meal, Sunni simply listened as Zakaria bared his soul. She had never heard her brother talk like this before. After he paid their bill, the two siblings stepped onto the sidewalk in front of the restaurant. Zakaria took his sister by the arm and hugged her warmly.

"I love you, Sunni."

The words shocked her, but not as much as what he said next.

"Have a great time at the Bible study tomorrow."

"Zakaria, how did you know I'm going to a Bible study?" Before he could answer, she added, "You won't tell Mom and Dad, will you?"

"Of course I won't. Your secret is safe with me. The reason I know about your Bible study is that it seems we have a mutual friend." He grinned. "Don't you just love Miriam?"

For Sunni, the surprises were just beginning. The next day at Bible study, Miriam started the lesson with a comment the dozen or so women found hard to comprehend.

"One of the reasons I was so attracted to following Jesus is because of the way He treated women. He honored them every chance He had. Did you know Jesus even allowed two women to be the first to discover His empty tomb after He rose from the dead? The men weren't there." Miriam punctuated her words with a broad smile. "Matthew 28 tells us the story. I'll read it to you now."

At the end of the two-hour Bible study, Sunni and Amina stayed to ask questions. Miriam answered each one from the Scriptures.

"But how do we know this Jesus is telling us the truth, Miriam? In my mind," Sunni challenged, "He has two strikes against Him. First, I'm sick of religion, and second, I'm sick of men and their promises."

Sunni was surprised when Amina spoke up first to her objections. "Well, maybe you should ask Jesus to prove Himself to you like I did. I prayed about a month ago to ask Jesus to prove Himself, and He has more than shown Himself to me since then."

"He has? What do you mean, Amina?"

"Jesus has come to me five times in my dreams. He's truly wonderful, Sunni. I hope you will meet Him soon."

A WORD FROM SUNNI

I did meet Jesus, even though He didn't come to me in a dream. I had a different introduction than Amina. I saw Him clearly in the lives of His followers. First it was through Miriam. She loved me the way I wished my own mother did. Then Amina embraced Jesus, and the changes in her were immediate. Then last—but most impressive—of all, Zakaria, who had been so cruel to me for years, was transformed as soon as he became a disciple of Jesus. For me, it took some time. After four marriages, I was broken inside; it was difficult for my heart to trust anyone—even Jesus Christ.

The decision was also difficult because Miriam had warned me about the cost. She pointed out the danger of coming from an observant Muslim family and from a small village.

"Living in Lebanon," she explained, "we are surrounded by hardline Muslims who would consider it an honor to kill you for leaving Islam. They would happily do that for your family. So before you even consider following Jesus: Are you willing to take up your cross and die for Him? This is what He did for you."

After wrestling with the decision for several months, I came to my senses and decided I would do the same for Him.

The religion I grew up in has many angry, violent people. Just a few miles from where I live, Christians are being crucified. The Islamic State fears no one and considers it open season on believers. They despise all Muslims who "defect." Some of my own cousins would be overjoyed to kill me because I love Jesus, and they may even succeed one day, but that does not concern me because meanwhile my life is worth living like never before.

First I was the barren wife *when I was married to Mustafa. Then I was the* beaten wife *married to Ghassan. Maged wanted me to be the* prostitute wife. *And finally, Hosni tried to make me his* slave wife. *My amazing Savior, though, has set me free from all my heartache, failures, and sin. Jesus has become a husband to me, which means I am now a* cherished wife. *I can hardly describe how much I love Him, and how astounding it is to know that He loves me unreservedly. I call Him "My Beloved."*

In my four marriages, I longed for a husband who would love me, but that was not to be. As believers, though, we are the bride of Christ, and Jesus is, beyond imagining, a giving, loving, honorable, and perfect *bridegroom. I no longer feel the need to be married in order to be happy and fulfilled. Jesus is sufficient. My question is: Whether you're married or not, is He sufficient for you?*

I tell everyone about my Jesus even though many believers have warned me to be more careful. But I just can't stop introducing people to Jesus. I've also found a new hero—or I should say, heroine—in the Bible. I'm just like the woman at the well in John 4. She went through many husbands before finding her one, true Love.

Because of Jesus' brutal death on the cross and His magnificent resurrection from the dead, I am free and forgiven. Jesus gave His life to you and me. I am in no way the same person I was before. I even found a small way to thank Him for what He's done for me: So that everyone I meet hears a snippet of the gospel, I changed my name. I was born into a Sunni *Muslim family, and my parents wanted to remind people of Islam every time they heard my name. But today people meet a different person. Now I'm Salaam. It means "peace," something I never had. Far too many Muslim women will never have this until they meet Jesus.*

The Middle East is unraveling with war. Killing sprees happen all around. But please remember this: I am your new friend from Lebanon, and I have perfect peace in my heart! Do you have this peace too?

Salaam in Jesus.

5 JUST THE USUAL DAMASCUS DEATH THREAT

W ill people want to kill us in al-Sweida like they did in Damascus, baba[1]?" Lina's concerned, twelve-year-old eyes probed her daddy's face for a hopeful answer. "That imam at the mosque near our house in Damascus always scared me!"

When the Yashou children asked questions of their father, he generally answered with a story. It was one of the traits that had long charmed Elisa Yashou about her husband. She wondered if the children loved Kareem's stories as much as she did and turned to the two children in the back seat of the family's Kia. She waved her hand theatrically toward the man driving. "And now, ladies and gentlemen: Kareem Yashou!"

Taking his cue, Kareem tipped his head, glanced in the rearview mirror, and gestured toward the emcee. "Let me tell you a story about the Druze people we're about to meet. *Their* story begins in the Old Testament, with Moses. God raised up that great prophet and leader of the Hebrews to guide the children of Israel into the Promised Land, and although Moses was born in Egypt, he married a woman named Zipporah who lived in the Midian desert with her father, Jethro. Once Moses had led God's people into the desert, Jethro gave Moses some great advice.

You'll recall there were more than two million Hebrews—far too many for one man to manage—so Jethro helped Moses figure out a leadership plan.

"What Jethro did for Moses became the pattern for Hebrew leadership for four centuries. In fact, some people thought what Jethro did was so great that, two thousand years later, they began a new religion and claimed Jethro was their first prophet."

Kareem checked the rearview mirror again to see if his audience was still following the story. "Do you know what the word *reincarnation* means?"

The two children shook their heads.

Kareem scanned the road ahead, then made eye contact in the mirror with the children. "In that case, I'll save the rest for another story. We're almost there."

The car exited Highway 110 from Damascus, swung into the old section of al-Sweida, and almost collided with a half dozen men in black pants bulging like sacks of grain from the waist to the knee.

"What's the deal with the baggy pants?" Hani Yashou snickered.

For a thousand years, newcomers to the Druze region had wondered about the grotesquely baggy pants common to adult men. Lina giggled at the sight of small white hats scrunched uncomfortably on each head and faces adorned with foot-long handlebar mustaches. Elisa raised an index finger to her lips. The little girl saw that the barest of smiles accompanied her mother's scowl.

"Baba, why did we move here?" Lina put her arms around her father's neck from the back seat and laid her head against his. At six foot three and 220 pounds, Kareem was her giant Arabic teddy bear. This time, Kareem didn't tell a story but did his next favorite thing. He sang in a deep baritone voice:

"Jesus, Name above all names, beautiful Savior, glorious Lord. Immanuel, God is with us . . ."

The other three Yashous joined in as the car rolled to a stop in front of their new home, sixty miles southwest of Damascus. Inside, it took less than an hour to unpack their few boxes and settle their meager belongings. It would take them much longer to get accustomed to the new world they had just entered.

"Why would a Christian family move to this neighborhood? It is for Druze people only. No Christians are allowed!"

The Yashous' first visitor stood at the front door as Kareem wondered why the man had even bothered to come by. Obviously, welcoming the new family was not on his agenda.

Kareem mustered a smile. "I thought Christians were free to live anywhere in Syria. Or has that changed recently? We are just leaving to get some dinner. Please come and join us with your family."

"My family will not be joining you for dinner tonight," the visitor spat back. "I have a long night of work ahead. Just know this, Kareem Yashou, I am watching every move you make. If you attempt to proselytize even a single Druze, we will arrest you immediately. We know your kind, and we know why you are here."

Kareem raised his eyebrows. Apparently, this man was not just any neighbor. In fact, Musa Fatah had already amassed a fat intelligence file. Secret police had bugged the Yashou family residence in Damascus and passed along the information to the local agent. Kareem had suspected the eavesdropping but was never able to find the listening devices.

Here in al-Sweida, Musa had one job and one job only—to keep Syria's religious groups out of each other's hair. The Assad regime believed the quickest way to destabilize Syria was to let a religious conflict fester. Disruptions always turned into full-fledged war, and Musa was determined that nothing in his area of influence would be allowed to contribute to such an event.

For Musa, keeping the peace between Druze and Alawites was usually little problem. Neither made any effort to convert the other. Druze and Alawites were born into the faith—or not. But the Christians were trouble—and so were the Sunnis. Sunnis threatened all other religious groups with a convert-or-die option, and that's why the Assad government had taken such pains through the years to keep them under control. Then the Syrian War began, and the regime lost most of its ability to restrain any of the groups as it fought for survival.

Musa, though, considered Christian leaders like Kareem more dangerous than anyone else. He regarded them as infiltrators who try to convert everyone—including Sunnis! Even as the Yashous drove out of Damascus, Musa had been ready. The day before he showed up at the door to "welcome" Kareem to town, he bugged the living room, kitchen, and master bedroom. Tiny RF audio transmitters would allow him to hear—and preempt—any plans the family might make to proselytize the good people of al-Sweida.

"Who was that, baba?" Lina looked up at the pillar of strength in her life as he walked back into the kitchen.

"It was just a man welcoming us to al-Sweida, Lina. I think

we've met before—he looked familiar." Kareem smiled at his daughter. "Let's go get something to eat."

The Yashous walked the few blocks downtown for their first Druze dinner. Neighbors stared as the family passed, but then looked away if noticed. On their way to dinner, Kareem reminded his family why they had come to al-Sweida.

"We've been talking about coming here for quite some time, but now that we're here, let me go over a few things about the Druze and why we want so much to help them. There are at least five hundred thousand of them in Syria. Some people say it's more like eight hundred thousand. For the most part, they're mountain people. Besides Syria, Druze also live in Lebanon, Israel, and Jordan. They're known for being warm and friendly, but generally, they are not open to a relationship with Jesus. You can see the fear in their eyes when you talk to them. I believe that's because, deep down, they suspect the Druze religion may be dead wrong.

"It can be a pretty difficult religion to follow. Especially because Druzis are not allowed to know much about their religion until they are forty years old. Even then, only the men learn the real secrets of the Druze religion. And if a Druze man were to leave the faith after age forty to become a follower of Jesus Christ—once he knows the secrets?" Kareem eyed each family member in turn. "That man would face certain death. It would also be a death sentence for the one who led him to Jesus.

"These people are confused about what they believe because they know so little about it, but one thing is for sure. They hate Muslims! If a Druze were to marry a Muslim, that, too, would be a reason to be killed, and the family would make sure the execution happened quickly.

"Ironically, the ultimate goal for Druze people is to find

peace and joy in this life. And since they believe in reincarnation, they hope that if they don't find tranquility in this life, they will in the next one by being *reincarnated*—or coming back to life—in another body of some sort. But do you know what?"

Lina and Hani shook their heads.

"They never find the peace they're looking for." Kareem smiled confidently. "And that's where the Yashou family comes in.

"Jesus appeared to me in a dream many months ago."

"Yes, baba. Tell us about the dream again." Lina reached for her daddy's hand.

Kareem held her hand warmly. "'Kareem,' Jesus said to me, 'I have chosen you to bring My love and My peace to a precious people.' He told me it was time for the Druze people to meet Him."

Kareem gently squeezed the small hand in his. "At first I didn't do anything, but a few days later, I told your mother about the experience. Before I could finish, she said Jesus had come to her in a dream the night before and showed her that He was calling us as a family to move to al-Sweida."

"So now that we are here, what are we supposed to do, baba?" Thirteen-year-old Hani stood ready to do whatever his hero asked him to do.

"Our mission is an easy one, my son. Pray for the Druze and love them. Jesus will do the rest."

The conversation ended as the foursome took the last empty patio table at the Jouzour Café. Kareem ordered a mixed grill, and the generous platter of kabobs arrived within minutes. By then, the Yashous had introduced themselves to a Druze family of six at the next table and were deep in conversation. Several minutes later, another family pulled up their chairs, and fifteen people sat in a circle. When Kareem began telling stories, the party started.

From his place in the corner by the kitchen door, the café owner usually took pleasure in watching his guests enjoy an evening at his restaurant. Seeing the assembly gathered around Kareem Yashou, though, he scowled and pulled a cell phone from his baggy pants. He pressed 1 on his speed dial.

A man answered on the first ring. "Musa Fatah here."

For Kareem the following morning, the Yashou party at Jouzour Café seemed a distant memory.

"It's as simple as this, Kareem. You can leave or stay, but if you stay, you will one day go to jail." Musa Fatah blew cigarette smoke at Kareem's face, adding to the years-old cigarette odor of the office.

His diet must be nothing but Nescafe and Afamias,[2] Kareem thought as he smiled at the government official with rancid breath and yellow teeth.

"What is my crime?" Kareem ignored the smoke swirling past his ears. "Did I break a law last night?"

"Don't get smart with me! You were talking to families in the restaurant about your religion—weren't you?"

"I promise that the subject of religion never entered the conversation."

Musa ignored his captor's defense. "Kareem, you are a threat to the Druze community."

"What—because I went to dinner and met a few new friends who introduced themselves to us first? That makes me a threat? Have you forgotten how hospitable most Druze are, Mr. Fatah?"

Musa snorted.

Two hours of unsubstantiated allegations and abusive threats later, Kareem stepped out of the office from his interview—as Musa had called it. As the security guard handed Kareem's cell phone back to him, it rang.

"Kareem, we've been praying, and I called the church back in Damascus. They are on their knees too. Are you in trouble?" Elisa sounded calm but spoke faster than usual.

"I'm fine, habibti. No problems here whatsoever. Musa thought we were talking religion all night with the Druze families. I told him not to worry, though, because I only talked about Jesus, not religion."

Elisa huffed. "Kareem, did you have to tell him so much in your first visit?"

"Yes, my sweet one." Kareem winced as he stepped into the midday sunlight. "I wanted to be honest with him. I even told him a story. He scowled at me the whole time, but I think he liked hearing about Zacchaeus. At one point, he smiled for an instant—just barely, but he did smile." Kareem grinned at the thought. "I'll be home in a few minutes."

A year after his first visit to Musa's office, Kareem was convinced his mission to al-Sweida had failed. He longed to see hundreds—or even thousands—of Druze follow Jesus. Yet more than twelve months and hundreds of friendly conversations into his mission, he could not count a single Druze neighbor who was the least bit interested in following Jesus. Polite and thoroughly cordial, his listeners simply stared blankly at him whenever the conversation turned to Jesus and how much He loved them. Kareem felt these people were as hard as steel about spiritual things.

He and Elisa had prayer-walked nearly every street in

al-Sweida. Every day they covered the neighborhoods in worship as they and the children sang in harmony along each street. They met in homes with acquaintances and new friends. But still, no response.

"Elisa, why did God call us here?" Kareem slumped on the living room floor, back against the couch. "Literally nothing has come of all our work here! These people have hearts like bricks, and there's no way to get through to them. I keep begging God to send dreams to the Druze just like the Muslims are receiving, but nothing happens no matter how I pray." He shook his head. "I admit, I'm defeated. God is going to have to find someone else to reach these people."

Kareem looked up as Elisa placed her hand on his left knee, then continued. "And it doesn't help that Musa's visits are getting more hostile. I almost wish he would just throw me in jail. He has no reason, though. What are they going to do—convict me for praying? Ha!

"I honestly don't know what to do next. Elisa, you and I have even fasted forty days and still nothing." He placed his hand on top of hers. "Maybe we should just go home."

When Lina and Hani arrived home from school at 3:30, their parents were still where they had left them—sitting on the living room floor, tears in their eyes. Kareem brushed his face with his hands, hoping to hide his true feelings from the two children, and launched into a story.

"The Druze men believe that one day a savior named Hakim will be born—and that a *man* will give birth to him! Whoever is chosen to be the birth-giver will not carry the child for nine months as a woman does. The baby will be conceived and born all at once."

Hani curled his lip at the thought.

"That's actually why they wear baggy pants. They don't want the newborn savior to fall on the ground!" Kareem chuckled. "Hard to believe, isn't it?"

The children plopped on either side of their father, Lina squeezing between Elisa and Kareem. Kareem wrapped an arm around each incredulous child.

"To us it seems silly, but a belief like that shows how desperate people are for a savior." He looked from Lina to Hani. "And that's why we are here. We want to shout it from the mountaintops that the Savior has already come." Kareem raised his eyebrows. "So far, though, I guess no one is listening to the message."

But Musa Fatah was listening. The audio transmission from the Yashou home spilled Kareem's vision from the speakers in Fatah's office. The man from the secret police relished the moment. What could be better? Kareem was a nonfactor in the community. No one cared. Musa's status quo was firmly in place. He laughed out loud at the defeated missionary.

"My daughter is sick, and I know that you pray to Jesus. I've heard Jesus can heal people." The visitor at the Yashous' front door looked sheepish. "Would He do this for my daughter?"

The 8:00 A.M. caller could have stepped out of a *National Geographic* article on "The Mountain Druze Men of Syria." For several seconds, Kareem stood speechless, absorbing the meaning of this novel encounter.

"Please tell me about your daughter. What is wrong with her?" Kareem's pastoral instincts sensed an opportunity and kicked into high gear.

Yazan Kasam began to cry as he spoke. "Jamilla is only twelve and has an advanced stage of cancer. The doctors say she will not live long." He sputtered. "She does not know this, of course." Tears sliced through the dust on his cheeks. "Could your Jesus heal her?"

Kareem was already asking himself the same question. His mind spun through possibilities—miraculous recovery as well as abject failure—as he placed a hand on the man's shoulder. He simply nodded and stepped out the front door of his house. As the mismatched pair walked down the street, Kareem's thoughts continued to race through his head.

Could Jesus heal her? Of course He could! Yet I have never seen anyone healed. Still, Jesus could do it if He wanted to. I've read about healings in the New Testament and heard about it happening even now. But I *haven't ever seen it.* Kareem's eyes drifted skyward as he walked. *Lord, give me faith to believe. If You were ever going to do something with the Druze, now would be the perfect time.*

At Yazan's house, Jamilla looked like a princess reclining on the living room couch. Her mother, Hala, sat close, supplying ice chips for her chronic dry mouth. Kareem's heart sank into his stomach. The merciless disease obviously owned the girl's body. A lump formed involuntarily in his throat at the sight of the pathetic girl in cheerful pink pajamas. The pastor smiled warmly at Jamilla but felt a tear roll down his cheek.

Jesus, You can do this. Of course You can do this. It was more of a pep talk to himself than a prayer. Finally: *Lord, I believe. Help my unbelief.*

With a deep breath, Kareem pulled a Bible from his coat pocket, dropped to his knees, and began to pray: "In the name of the Lord Jesus I come before You, heavenly Father. I ask

You to touch Jamilla with the resurrection power that raised Jesus from the dead. This dear family is crying out to You. So, together, we ask You, Lord, to say once again *talitha koum! Little girl, arise!*"

Kareem was inspired by his own words and prayed with Arabic passion. Yazan, Hala, and two brothers gaped at Kareem. They had never seen praying like this. Smiling, Jamilla fixed an angelic gaze on the man who prayed for her.

After several minutes, Kareem rose slowly to his feet, head still bowed. Without opening his eyes, he asked, "How do you feel, Jamilla?"

The little girl sat up. "I think I feel the same, but I am so warm. Can we open a window?"

Kareem's human emotions tried to topple the deep faith in his heart. *I believe, Jesus. I still believe, Jesus.*

After the prayer, Hala invited Kareem into the kitchen for tea. The family shared two pots around the table as Yaza, Hala, and the boys each thanked Kareem and tapped their chests in a silent gesture to say how Kareem's prayer had touched their hearts.

"Mr. Yashou, I cannot recall ever seeing anything like that in my life." Yazan held back tears.

"What do you mean, Yazan?"

"I mean the way you prayed. You have a strong faith in God." He nodded. "I wish mine were that strong. We've been praying for Jamilla for a long time, and maybe our prayer will not be answered in this lifetime." His voice trailed off.

Kareem leaned toward Yazan and whispered, "Can you please explain what you're thinking?"

"Maybe Jamilla will have a short life . . . the first time. We believe God is the ultimate judge, and He sees her innocence. We can only hope that Jamilla is reincarnated into a strong healthy woman next time." Yazan raised his head mustering confidence.

Kareem considered for several seconds how to respond. "Yazan, I believe in something better than reincarnation. I believe in the resurrection. I—"

A fist pounding on the front door halted the introduction to Kareem's story.

Hala scurried into the living room and opened the door. "Musa Fatah!"

Kareem cringed at Hala's greeting.

"It's great to see you again," Hala continued. "Would you and your friends like to have some tea with us and Pastor Kareem?"

"Actually, I'm very busy today, but I would like to have some *words* with Reverend Kareem."

Kareem rolled his eyes and headed for the front door.

After a quiet walk down the block to Musa's office, Kareem broke the silence and seated himself for another interview.

"So what is the reason for our visit?"

Musa answered with a slap across Kareem's face. Two goons stood behind Musa, watching Kareem's face for any sign of weakness. Musa slammed a file folder on his desk and fired a half dozen questions at Kareem before the dazed pastor could answer.

"So now you are visiting the Druze in their homes in hopes of proselytizing them. Is that right?" Musa cared nothing for answers. He wanted only a quick confession out of his most-wanted evangelist.

Kareem sat up straight and shouted into the barrage of inquiries. "I have good news for you, Mr. Fatah! The family invited me to come and pray for them. They have a sick daughter and hope Jesus will heal her. Would you like me to pray for you and your friends as well?"

The goon on Musa's right slammed an open palm into Kareem's left cheek. As Kareem reeled with the first slap, the second goon blasted the pastor's right cheek, sending him reeling back in the other direction.

Musa growled, "That's one thing I don't need, Mr. Yashou, is *your* prayers. But if your God is listening, you better start praying for yourself right now and plead for His mercy. You won't get any from us. This is going to be a very long day for you because it's time you learned a lesson! The Syrian government will *not* allow anyone to destabilize the Druze people. Do you understand me?" Musa sneered at Kareem, his face inches from the pastor's.

"We have enough problems without you trying something foolish like starting a church in this city. If you do, we will shut it down. We will shut it down! Do you hear me? And we will throw you out of al-Sweida. You will never return! And that would be the greatest kindness we could offer you. Yazan Kasam's relatives will probably kill you one day if you try to convert him. The Druze do not waffle on such things like Muslims do. They kill converts, Mr. Yashou—*and* the ones doing the converting. This is how it happens: One day you will be fine, and then . . . no one will ever hear from you again. A private killing keeps things 'in the family,' you might say."

Musa threw his head back as if on a hinge and laughed toward the ceiling. The goons roared with him, then began beating Kareem.

Between blows, Musa screamed meaningless questions in Kareem's face. Kareem laughed to himself, noting that Musa's breath was more torturous than the goons' fists and rods.

By quitting time that afternoon, his government job done for the day, Musa adjourned the session. "I'm starved, and since it is dinner time . . ." He feigned courtesy. "That will be enough for today. I hope we have the pleasure of seeing you again, Mr. Yashou."

Kareem winced at the searing stripes across his back as he put his coat back on. Eyes black and blue, he headed into the cool evening air and up the street toward home.

Halfway to his house, the cell phone in his jacket buzzed. Elisa's nerves calmed as the call went through, and she was finally greeted with the sound of Kareem's voice. He was singing.

A week later, Elisa dabbed antibiotic cream over the wounds on her husband's back, thankful that he no longer grimaced at her touch. "Kareem, I can't figure out God in all this. He didn't heal Jamilla, and then you receive the beating of your life. I can see being persecuted when God is moving in power among the people, but He isn't!"

A knock at the door interrupted Kareem's attempt to gather his thoughts and respond. Elisa stood from the couch, re-tied her apron as she walked across the room, and opened the green metal front door. She took several steps back and turned toward Kareem, hand over her mouth, eyes wide open.

From his seat on the couch, Kareem could not see the visitor but, gauging his wife's reaction, made the logical assumption. *When is Musa going to give me a break?* he wondered. *I'm not even healed from the last beating. Is it time for another one?*

Speechless, Elisa motioned Kareem to come to the door. Pulling on his shirt, he joined his wife. His jaw dropped at what he saw. Musa Fatah wasn't the problem. In fact, there didn't seem to be a problem at all. More than fifty Druze acquaintances stood peacefully in a line from the Yashou porch to the street.

At the front of the line, an elderly man turned to his wife sitting in a wheelchair beside him. "My wife is paralyzed on her left side by a stroke." He looked plaintively at Kareem. "Will you pray to Jesus for her?"

Kareem and Elisa looked at each other, then back at the line of al-Sweida neighbors.

Kareem didn't know the name of the man who had asked the question. "Sir, why would you ask me to pray for your wife? I don't understand."

About halfway to the street a man broke from the line and headed for Kareem. It was Yazan Kasam. "Did you not hear the news, Mr. Yashou? I thought sure you had." A grin erupted across the width of his face. "Jamilla is well! The doctors in Damascus said her cancer is gone." The grin disappeared, and he choked on his words.

Stunned, Kareem looked again at Elisa. A laugh from the crowd drew their attention back to the front yard as a girl in a bright pink dress ran giggling to the Yashous' front steps. Jamilla Kasam leaped onto Kareem. As the healthy twelve-year-old hugged the man who had prayed for her, Yazan, Kareem, and Elisa sobbed with joy and gratitude.

Cheers exploded from the crowd gathered in front of the Yashou house, and the accompanying applause lasted for several minutes. Druze women raised their faces toward the sky and squealed a customary howl of celebration.

As the cacophony subsided, Yazan launched into the story of Jamilla's recovery. "It was time for Jamilla's checkup a few days after you visited our home. She told us she was feeling better, but we didn't think much about it since she has good days and bad. When we arrived at the Shami Hospital in Damascus, they did a battery of tests, the usual blood work, and after that, the scans. We got worried when we saw a team of doctors and nurses huddled outside of Jamilla's room, discussing the results. Hala and I prepared ourselves for bad news.

"But, instead, Kareem, God answered your prayers! Your Jesus did it! The cancer is completely gone! The doctors were mystified over its sudden disappearance. I'm sorry I did not have the faith you did during your prayer. Other people have prayed for Jamilla as well, but I guess their problem is that they never prayed to Jesus." He shook his head. "This Jesus is amazing. You prayed to Him just one time, and now the cancer is all gone? This is hard for us to fathom."

Without giving Kareem a chance to respond, Yazan swept his right hand toward the people on the Yashous' sidewalk. "Mr. Yashou, will Jesus heal my friends too?"

Kareem hugged Elisa, then Hani and Lina who had heard the commotion and joined their parents at the front door. Then the pastor darted inside and returned with his Bible. The Yashous began the ad hoc front yard prayer service with a song:

"Jesus, Name above all names, beautiful Savior, glorious Lord. Immanuel, God is with us . . ."

More than an hour later, twenty people had been prayed over as desperate families watched. No one's symptoms changed immediately, but Kareem persisted. Yazan stood by Kareem's side and prayed along with him.

Finally, Yazan raised his arms toward the Druze families and hollered, "You must believe that Jesus can do this! Pray with Mr. Yashou and also believe in your heart!"

He turned toward Kareem, eyes wide. "Is it okay that I say this to them?"

Kareem squeezed his eyes shut and bear-hugged Yazan. "You can say that all you want!"

Once everyone who asked had received prayer, a latecomer showed up at the back of the line. Kareem called to him. "Musa! It's very nice to see you. Are you going to ask for Jesus to touch you too?"

Yazan Kasam could not contain his excitement and beckoned the representative of the secret police to join them on the porch. Musa Fatah, though, could not contain his disgust and spat on the ground.

"No, I don't need anything myself, but thank you, Yazan."

"But I insist, Musa. Kareem must pray to Jesus for you too. Kareem, will you?"

"Of course I will, Yazan!" Kareem closed his eyes and spoke so the whole crowd could hear. "Father, I thank You for my friend Musa. He is a good man that does his job well. I can certainly attest to that!"

Kareem opened his eyes and winked at Musa, who rolled his eyes.

"I don't know exactly what Musa needs—or his family—but in the name of Jesus, I ask for You to give generously to this man, Lord. He needs You in his life. If they are in need of anything, would You provide it for the Fatah family?"

When Kareem opened his eyes again, Musa was walking alone up the street in the direction of his office.

In the days that followed, spiritual power from the Yashou home rippled through al-Sweida and several surrounding Druze villages. The woman in the wheelchair was up and walking. A man unable to shake a severe case of shingles woke up the morning after Kareem's prayer to find them gone. A woman suffering from excruciating abdominal spasms was now pain-free.

Kareem and Elisa decided to keep a record of these divine interventions, and a spiral notebook began to travel with them wherever they went. If a miracle occurred, they recorded and numbered it. Because of the powerful outpouring, Kareem and Elisa now led people to Christ almost daily. Kareem trained new converts to tell God's story from the Bible and also to tell the story of their own salvation experience.

When believers visited periodically from Damascus, Kareem glowed with stories of how God was working among the Druze. But when the visitors called Kareem a modern-day apostle Paul, Kareem hung his head, spoke softly, and barely made eye contact. The humble man who had never seen a miracle of God became known as the man who prayed, and the hand of God moved.

Even Musa Fatah could not stop the Druze awakening. He suspended his visits with Kareem and merely watched from a distance. He also stopped using the listening devices in Kareem's home to gain information and simply listened in on the Yashou family evening prayers.

"Lahoud, did you get kicked in the face by a soccer ball or something?" Hani stopped his friend in the school hallway on his way back to class after lunch.

"I did get kicked in the face—but it wasn't a soccer ball. It was my father's foot. He was drunk again last night." The teen boy's shoulders drooped. "My face isn't the only bruise I have—and you should see my mom." He paused, a new thought entering his mind. "Hani, do you think your father would come and pray for my father?"

That night, Lahoud's father, Nihad Salman, hurled obscenities at Kareem. When he picked up his teacup and threw it at Kareem, Elisa and Lahoud's mother, Ronza, escorted their children out of the Salman living room. At the front door, Elisa glanced back at Kareem. He mouthed one word to her: "Demons."

Outside, Ronza broke into tears. "He's like this almost every night." The forty-two-year-old Druze woman had given up hope.

Inside, the confrontation was on. Kareem read aloud from the Bible: "For our struggle is not with flesh and blood but with the rulers . . . Nihad, I believe Jesus wants to set you free tonight. Will you let me pray with you?"

"Never!" Nihad charged across the room at Kareem.

"In the name of the Lord Jesus, enemies of Christ, leave Nihad now!"

The crazed man fell to his knees as if he had been shot. He rocked forward and howled through tears, "Help me, Kareem! Pray to Jesus for my soul!"

Kareem read scriptures and prayed for an hour with Nihad. When the two men finished, peace fell over the Salman home. Before Elisa and Kareem left, Ronza and the three Salman children also gave their lives to Jesus. The Yashou family floated home that night.

"Baba, the words that came out of Mr. Salman's mouth were creepy!" Lina reached for Kareem, and he swept her into his arms. "Are the demons gone for good?"

"Lina, the devil tries to make us afraid. He lost the fight with

Jesus a long time ago, though, and he just won't admit it. Jesus sealed the devil's fate, and we must stand our ground against him. Mr. Salman will probably sleep like a baby tonight." He smiled at his daughter. "Maybe we can too."

The next evening, the Yashous walked to the Salman home. This time, instead of being greeted with Nihad's cursing, it was Lahoud playing the lute that they heard upon approaching.

As Ronza ushered the Yashous into the living room, Lahoud announced, "I've been working on some songs today. I read from the Bible you gave us last night, Mr. Yashou, starting in the Psalms that you told us about. This song is from number 23."

Kareem suspected Lahoud's music was the most beautiful sound ever to come out of the Salman home. Within an hour, neighbors began dropping in to see if the Salmans were hosting a party. But it was not a party. It was the first church meeting of the al-Sweida Druze believers.

For them, it was a community Pentecost. Each night after Lahoud's first performance of Psalm 23, the Salman home welcomed neighbors and relatives for singing and Bible study. During the day, Kareem taught the Bible to Nihad and trained him for several hours in evangelism and discipleship.

People were drawn to Nihad's remarkable transformation. Most of the neighbors couldn't remember the last time they had seen the once-wild man sober. They would never again see him drunk. Attendance at the Salman church grew nightly, and two weeks after Nihad's deliverance, the Salman home overflowed as a new group leader began to teach.

"Jesus said, 'I have come that you might have life, and that you might have it in abundance.'" Nihad spoke confidently for his first teaching session.

"Life has come to the city of al-Sweida. Jesus' message is for all of us, and with this message comes responsibility. He has come not just for the few families that gathered here tonight but for all the Druze."

Nihad unrolled a map of Syria and held it toward the group. "Every village around al-Sweida needs to hear the news that God has come to *us*. Let me show you a simple plan of how we can take Jesus' love to the rest of our people all over Druze Mountain. Jesus has called us to a holy journey that we must make together. He wants us to go two by two to each village and search for a person of peace. It's part of His plan to make disciples, just like He did in the first century."

Nihad pointed to a spot on the map. "Our first town to pray for is Hadar."

Hadar became the first of several dozen Druze villages affected by Nihad's prayer plan. Within six months, churches were meeting in homes, and Druze villages were seeing new followers of Christ. Nihad became the first Druze pastor, Kareem continued to pray, and God continued working miracles. Believers visited from Jordan, Egypt, Iraq, and America to see firsthand Jesus' breakthrough with the Druze. And no longer a place to be avoided, the Nihad home became the place to be nearly every night of the week. Lahoud composed Druze praise songs from Scripture and led sweet worship with his lute.

The reports of Druze following Jesus were not welcomed by traditional religious leaders, however. A fatwa was issued on

Kareem. Persecution broke out, and one nonbelieving village even threatened to attack the Druze converts in al-Sweida. The unchanging community of Druze had never witnessed anything like this, and the growing instability proved too much for Musa Fatah. After months of ignoring Kareem, he invited the pastor in for an interview.

"Mr. Yashou, I have an official document from my supervisors." Musa stood over Kareem, who sat in the same chair in which he had received the beating more than six months earlier.

"As of today, Kareem, you and your family no longer live in al-Sweida. If you stay, you will be sent to prison, so don't even think about it. If I had my way, you would be serving time already.

"The stir in the villages has reached the capital city, and news of the contract on your life has not gone unnoticed. Did you know that if someone kills you, a reward of $10,000 will be paid to your murderer? I only wish I could collect!

"If you and your family are not gone by 5:00 P.M. today, you will be taken immediately to prison. Do I make myself clear, Kareem Yashou?"

Musa offered Kareem no recourse, and the Yashous' kitchen clock read 3:00 P.M. by the time Kareem returned home with the news that it was moving day. Elisa and the children sat, stunned, in their living room at the thought that they had only two hours to pack and leave town for good.

"This was to be expected," Kareem reassured the family. "When the miracles began, and God started healing the sick, that was one thing. But now, Nihad says there are four hundred Druze believers. The Druze pastors will replace us." He smiled peacefully. "Now it's their turn to lead."

By 4:30, news of the Yashous' imminent departure had

spread among local believers. By the time Kareem started loading the Kia sedan, his front yard overflowed with men in white caps and baggy pants as well as women and children bearing farewell gifts and pita sandwiches. At 4:45, Kareem motioned the group to gather by his front steps. Lahoud played one last worship song for the Yashou congregation, and Kareem prayed over his flock. Men and women alike broke into tears as they shared parting hugs.

With minutes to go, Kareem, Elisa, Hani, and Lina, tears still drying on their cheeks, drove silently away from their home. The applause and howling of the neighbors receded as Hani and Lina waved out the back window at their friends. They had been here less than two years, but al-Sweida would never be the same.

Just past the Highway 110 traffic circle a mile north of al-Mazr'aa Street, Lina, still staring listlessly out the back window, startled. "Baba, who are those men driving behind us? There are two cars coming toward us—fast."

Kareem checked the rearview mirror and thought of the $10,000 reward on his head. He gunned the Kia up the straight stretch of road, but Kareem's pursuers closed the gap between them and the Yashou car.

Glancing from the road to the rearview mirror and back, Kareem's eyes widened. "Everyone down! They have weapons!"

An arm extended from the passenger side of the lead car behind them and fired several blasts from a semi-automatic pistol. Bullets pinged off the trunk of the Kia.

"I don't think I'll be able to outrun them," Kareem shouted, half to himself. "Lord, we need a miracle! This time for my family!"

Several shots zipped past the windows while a few lodged in the trunk of the car. As the predators inched closer, Kareem studied the road ahead, sizing up his options.

"I think I see our miracle. Thank You, Lord Jesus!"

A tenth of a mile ahead, two tractor-trailer trucks, one in the left lane and one in the right, approached the next traffic circle. Kareem accelerated into the right lane, then swung left between the trucks just as they reached the traffic circle.

"Kareem!" Elisa screamed as the Kia shimmied between the trucks and skidded around the north side of the traffic circle, the trucks screening his movement from the cars behind. He careened into the southbound lane as the two chase cars flew past on the other side of the traffic circle. Barely slowing, Kareem slid the car into a right turn at the first road he came to, and sped away from the main highway.

A half mile up the road, Elisa, still white-faced, turned slowly toward her husband. "Who were they, Kareem?" She reached over the seat to pat the children who were still on the floor.

"They may have been Druze militia—or maybe just someone trying to rob us." He smiled playfully at Elisa. "I think we'll take a few scenic back roads to Damascus."

In the capital city, the Yashous reconnected with fellow believers, and within days, Kareem resumed his ministry to the underground church and its Sunni Muslim Background Believers. The death threats also began the week Kareem returned to the city.

A month after leaving al-Sweida, Kareem prayed late one afternoon as he walked the ancient Straight Street[3] in old town Damascus, the Islamic call to evening prayers battling for his attention. It took several seconds before he recognized a different sound between stanzas blaring from the mosque loudspeakers.

"Kareem! Kareem!"

The voice came from behind him, familiar but not threatening. He turned toward the sound and froze.

"Kareem! It's good to see you!"

Kareem just stared in response as Musa Fatah approached.

"I hope you have no hard feelings, Kareem. There was never anything personal between you and me. I was merely doing my job." Musa might as well have been reuniting with an old friend.

"You *beat* me, Musa," Kareem said slowly.

The man looked puzzled but smiled at Kareem. "Of course I did! It was my job. Intimidation is all part of it. The problem is, it never seemed to have any effect on you—and that's why I respected you, Kareem."

Musa stopped three feet from Kareem. His breath still reeked.

"I'm glad that you got out of al-Sweida, but did you have to come back to Damascus?" Musa shook his head. "The death threats here are from Muslims, not Druze, and the ISIS operatives won't send you a warning notice like our government did, Kareem. I'm worried about you. They'll cut your head off and ask questions later." He pointed at Kareem. "You need to get out of this city—soon."

That was a genuine, friendly warning, and not a threat. Kareem let the thought register before he spoke.

"Musa. There's something I've wanted to give to you for a long time." He reached in the pocket of his jacket. "It's a Bible— and before you say no, please hear me out."

Musa cocked his head and pulled a cigarette from his lips. "What makes you think I don't want it? I hoped you would give me one. I've always wondered what is in the Bible. I just want to know why you waited so long." Musa smiled and blew smoke up in the air, this time avoiding Kareem's face.

"Musa," Kareem sighed, "you've been following me for years. You harass me and probably have bugged my house again. Is all of that over, or are you still going to be my shadow?"

Musa flicked cigarette ash on the sidewalk. "Of course I'll keep following you, Kareem. That's still my job. But thank you for the Bible. My family is Muslim, yet I will begin reading it with them *tonight*. And before I go, I want to tell you something. When you prayed for me the day all the Druze came to your home, I felt something. There's a power when you pray, and I want to find out what it is." He nodded, his face serious. "However, I must go now." Musa extended a hand toward Kareem.

Touched by Musa's warmth, Kareem shook the policeman's hand for the first time in the two years since they'd met.

"Musa, after you read the Bible this week, do you want to meet for coffee so we can talk about what you're reading?"

Musa eyed his cigarette respectfully and tossed it on the sidewalk. He crushed it beneath the toe of his black shoe, and then looked Kareem in the eye.

"Well . . . yes . . . I think I would like that very much."

But Kareem's first handshake with the man from the secret police was also his last.

A WORD FROM KAREEM

It came as a shock for me to find out that two days later Musa Fatah was dead. I am the one that was supposed to be killed in Damascus and al-Sweida, not him. He was out for a morning cup of coffee and got caught in crossfire between Bashar Al-Assad's military and ISIS. He didn't stand a chance.

My family attended the funeral, so I could pay my respects. I can only hope that in those two days after I gave him the Bible, he came to understand Jesus and the glorious grace that can save anyone. I thought I might see a miracle on Straight Street where a Saul was transformed into a Paul, but it was not to be.

Musa is a tragic example of how short life can be in Syria. Here, the life expectancy for men has dropped twenty years since the beginning of the war. Seventy-five used to be the average; now a fifty-five-year-old man is considered old.

I don't know how long I will live, but every day is a gift. Who knows what the Lord will do with any of us in our next day? I know, though, that when your goal is to please Him above all else, and not yourself, you will see miracles! The Druze were an unreached people group, but God gathered them into His family. I can still hardly believe God did miracles through me who had never seen a miracle of any kind.

Although I once struggled to believe Him, now I have pages of miracles done among the Druze. God stands ready to do the miraculous. But the question is: Are we ready? Do we long for His power more than anything? If we thirst to see Jesus worshipped by those who don't yet know Him, then I guarantee you will see the miraculous. It may not be healings like I saw, but you will see the hand of God in people's lives.

I encourage you to make that your quest in life—to see Jesus do the miraculous. I ask Him now every day for exactly that. If you join me in asking this of God, it will transform how you think and how you live. I'm proof of that.

A WORD FROM TOM ABOUT KAREEM

My friend Kareem will never say this because he would worry that in some way it might take the focus off of Jesus, but Kareem and his family saw more than ninety people healed. Jamilla was the first, but there were many more. I saw Jesus touch people several times through Kareem, and since I know where he keeps his spiral notebook, it's the first thing I look for whenever I visit him. Although Kareem had never seen anyone healed of so much as a cold, miraculous healings from cancer, diabetes, paralysis, brain tumors, multiple sclerosis, and more brought the breakthrough the Druze needed. But what makes Kareem smile more than anything is to see a Druze sharing Jesus with another Druze. It's not just happening in the Druze villages by the way. They were unreached, but now the Druze have sent missionaries to . . . are you ready for this? Saudi Arabia and Brazil!

I pray for Kareem every day. Would you join me? He has a bull's-eye on his back because he is mighty in the hand of God in a country falling apart at the seams. Kareem, Elisa, Hani, and Lina have brought hope to Syrians—whether Druze, Muslims, Alawites, or believers in Christ. Thanks to Kareem's faithfulness and competent training of Druze leaders, as of this writing, more than two thousand Druze have become Jesus followers. So pray for Kareem and his family. He is a marked man—but he's not leaving no matter how many threats he receives.

6 THE ISIS RECRUIT FROM MOSUL

*M*osul.

Faisal Radi turned the city name over in his head, relishing its significance. *Soon it will be the center of the world.*

He squinted down the sun-scorched street alongside Nur al-Din, the Great Mosque of Mosul, Iraq, scanning the sweltering horde scuttling like workers from a monstrous ant colony into Friday prayers on this first week of Ramadan 2014. The smothering, still air made the women in black burqas on the streets feel like a piece of pita bread straight out of the oven. Yet, the 108-degree heat kept no one from being at the event that had the city buzzing even though none had had any water since before sunrise. The Great Mosque was crammed full of bodies and there was electricity in the air. Faisal wondered how many might faint—and how many might be crushed if they did. He checked his watch impatiently. *Almost noon.*

As he looked up again, a face emerged from the crowd.

"Medo! I told you to hurry. We should have been here an hour ago!" Faisal grabbed the arm of his lifelong friend and pulled him toward the mosque entrance.

"If the new caliph makes his appearance today and July 4,

2014, becomes the most important date in history, I'll always remember that you made us late for the big event."

"Oh Faisal! You wear me out with all your worrying. At least we've made it inside the mosque."

The two men in their twenties wedged themselves into the crowd pressed inside the cavernous mosque, many of the hundreds of similar age, and claimed standing room at the base of an inner archway supporting the nine-hundred-year-old building. Although a mere two feet from Medo's ear, Faisal raised his voice to be heard over the cacophony around them.

"What was so important that you couldn't get to it later this afternoon, Medo?"

Medo sneered at his friend's continued chiding, his answer at first seeming to ignore the question. "Ramadan is brutal in Iraq, isn't it? No water until sundown in this heat? It's crazy." He paused, looking Faisal in the eye. "If you must know, I was praying and preparing myself for the big day—for *this*!"

The answer seemed to make Faisal feel better. His face relaxed.

"This is a new era, Medo. Sunni Muslims all over the world have dreamed of this for centuries. If our new leader arrives, the caliphate will restart *today*." He raised his hands triumphantly. "The Ottomans may have lasted four hundred years, but this one will outlive them because *they* were Turks. Everyone knows the leadership of Islam is only truly legitimate when people of Mohammad's Arabic heritage are in control. The Prophet entrusted *us* to lead all Muslims of the world!"

In his excitement, Faisal almost shouted. Nearby heads turned to see the ad hoc preacher. Several nearby listeners caught Faisal's eye and nodded approval. Medo chuckled at his friend's reception, then turned to an immediate, pragmatic consideration. By the archway, they had carved out enough space to stand within earshot of the minbar.[1] When it came time to pray on their knees, though, they would have to get creative—aggressive—and push for more room.

Thinking about the immediate issue of enough space to kneel also took Medo's mind off of the far more compelling and long-term concerns that churned in his gut. He wished he shared his best friend's unfettered optimism over the events unfolding around them. Having been friends since they were preschoolers, the two men knew each other so well they could finish each other's thoughts. Yet Medo dared not reveal his thoughts today.

Faisal, envisioning only life as a soldier for the caliphate, would not comprehend the turmoil in Medo's heart. Regardless of who controlled the state, Medo had radically different aspirations. In the three weeks since the Islamic State had begun its occupation of Mosul, the city had become nearly unrecognizable. The new regime had closed down the university where Medo had been pursuing his dream of a degree in pharmaceutical science. Ever since Medo was a boy, he wanted nothing more than to help people. He dreamed of discovering a cure for cancer or perhaps a protocol to stem the tide of the Type 2 diabetes surging among the Arabs of the Middle East. While many of his college-bound friends had headed to the University of Baghdad, Iraq's largest university, Medo focused his dreams on the more prestigious medical college at the University of Mosul. So the real reason Medo had been late to the mosque was that he could barely force himself to come support this beginning-of-the-end of his personal dreams.

Just one month before, the University of Mosul was one of the most influential educational and research centers in the Middle East. But when the Islamic State made the university its headquarters, new campus leadership boasted that more than eight thousand books had been destroyed as well as some one hundred thousand manuscripts. The greater wisdom of ISIS dictated that the campus needed a *cleansing* if it were to serve as the Islamic State's new capitol. Revised college courses would be announced shortly and the new faculty introduced. Meanwhile, students had no further educational responsibilities until the changes were made public. All of Medo's and Faisal's summer classes were cancelled. The one remaining responsibility for students was to register for service in the ISIS military.

As if the incineration of his educational dreams weren't enough, Medo also feared for his family—especially his sisters. In one of its most despicable moves, ISIS had begun applying its "theology of rape" as an excuse to abuse the women of Mosul. According to ISIS leadership, all women were fair game for those "in the fight," and even girls under age ten were forced into so-called marriage with ISIS soldiers. As a result, the female population largely cowered in their homes.

To Medo, the most grievous spectacle had become the absurd mistreatment of Christians. Even though Mosul was 90 percent Sunni Muslim, it had maintained and encouraged its reputation as a center for Christianity in the Middle East. Since the first century AD, Armenians and Assyrians had a secure home here. Yazidis and Kurds also lived amenably in this spiritual and ethnic puzzle that worked like few places in the Middle East. But June 2014 marked a turning point in this history of Mosul. ISIS burned to the ground dozens of churches—many of them centuries old. Yazidi women had become special targets for use as sex slaves. It appeared as if no other religion would ever again be tolerated in Mosul. And non-Muslims were not the only ones to suffer. Any form of Islam that did not comply strictly with the Islamic State's ideology was forbidden. Mosul had fallen.

Suddenly the clamor around Medo dwindled to a deathly quiet, the change startling Medo from his thoughts. He followed the gaze of a thousand eyes as they watched Abu Bakr al-Baghdadi ascend the minbar. The leader of the world's richest terrorist group stood at the microphone, nearly unmoving, for almost a minute as he scanned the crowd. Under his command, ISIS had become too radically vicious even for the fundamentalists in al-Qaeda. In fulfillment of his plan earlier this year, he formally broke from the terrorist group that in his eyes had grown soft.

The Baghdadi followers gathered in Nur al-Din gazed, awestruck, at their revered leader. There had not been so much as a photograph of him in public since 2009. For four of the five intervening years, Baghdadi had refined his concept of Islam in a US detention camp in Iraq. On the day he was set free, Baghdadi reportedly mocked his American captors with a parting threat: "I'll see you in New York."

"Medo," Faisal whispered, his hand across his mouth directing the words toward his friend, "can you believe it? He's here. The caliphate has begun, and we're a part of it."

Eyes on the bearded man at the minbar, Faisal dropped his hand and stood at attention as Baghdadi addressed the crowd:

> So take advantage of this noble month, O worshipper of Allah! Fight therein. This is the month in which the Prophet commanded armies to fight against the enemies of Allah.

The month in which he would wage jihad against the poly-theists! So fear Allah, O slaves of Allah.

O Muslims! Allah, the Blessed and Exalted, created us to single Him out in monotheism, and to establish His all-encompassing way of life. He, the exalted, said: "I did not create the jinn and mankind except to worship me."

And Allah likes us to kill his enemies, and make jihad in his sake. He, the Exalted, said: "Fighting has been enjoined upon you while it is hateful to you."

And He, the Exalted, said: "And fight them until there is no fitnah[2] and [until] the religion, all of it, is for Allah. And if they cease—then indeed, Allah is Seeing of what they do."

O people! The religion of Allah be just in it, stand up for it, and affirm its truthfulness, and do not stray from what Allah has given us. Be firm with the sharia of Allah, and the reference to it, and apply and accept of hudud. . . . [3]

And this is the application of the religion of Allah. And this is the Book that gives guidance, and the sword that delivers swift victories.[4]

Medo cut his eyes toward Faisal and studied his friend's rapt attention, trying not to let his own panic at the caliph's shocking words show on his face. The life-altering maelstrom blowing through the blended city on the plains of Nineveh had, in three weeks, consumed most of Mosul's citizens. And Medo could see from al-Baghdadi's message that reversing course was not an option. ISIS had thrust Mosul far past the point of no return. Some, like Faisal, reveled in the expectation of a new life. Others more like Medo would begin to understand the horrors in store after today's call to prayer.

Like it or not (and he certainly did *not* like it), Medo was now a soldier of the Islamic State. At first, he had assumed the best about the coming of Daesh.[5] For young Iraqis like Medo, national pride had all but been destroyed by the war in Iraq. The cycle of violence and continual humiliation of Iraq before the world caused a mass exodus from the country Medo loved. Now that America had abandoned the country and Iraqi leadership was in the hands of the Shia government, the disaster had to be sorted out by the people of Iraq.

Earlier this spring, Medo had thought the Islamic State would do just that. Sunni Islam would control Iraq once again as it did under Saddam Hussein. So during the fall of Mosul the previous month, Medo, too, had waved flags and welcomed the Islamic State. In the three weeks since, though, he had seen a transformation from the growing decency of coexistence to inconceivable brutality crushing anyone outside the ISIS version of Islam. His hopes transformed to desperation, Medo's stomach churned at the thought of what might be the worst still to come.

On July 4, 2014, the self-proclaimed caliph demonstrated his control of the most feared Islamic group in the world, and on July 5, Medo witnessed the beginning of unspeakable crimes launched by the Islamic State against Christians, Yazidis, and any Muslims who disrespected the new leadership. Although Faisal and Medo would serve side by side, just as they had in everything since their youth, their hearts were no longer of one accord. The venomous propaganda had poisoned Faisal while Medo began to plot how he could escape—and how to survive if he succeeded.

During the week after al-Baghdadi's sermon, dozens of non-compliant citizens were decapitated in streets throughout the city. On their walk home after the next Friday prayers, Medo cautiously probed Faisal to assess his friend's view of the week's events and his loyalty to the caliph.

"So, Muslims beheading Muslims. Does that track with your thinking?"

"Of course Muslims are being killed. They deserve it. The religion many have followed for years does not even remotely reflect the pure Sharia law we are now blessed with. It is good to start by purging our own ranks. Once that's done, we will destroy the Christians and Yazidis too. I cannot wait to see Christian blood all over the streets! It is time they leave our city. This transformation to the Islamic State is historic! And there is no place for Christians here."

Faisal's virulent opinions were new to Medo. How could they have been friends for so long and Medo not seen this coming?

"But Faisal, my dear friend, some of *our* friends we grew up with—and even played soccer with—are Assyrian Christians. Do you want to kill them as well?" Medo was careful to speak without emotion.

"Yes! Of course I do." Medo felt a pain in his stomach as Faisal sneered. "They don't belong here anymore. But our great leader is a man of peace, you know. He may even offer for them to stay if they convert to Islam or are willing to pay the jizya tax for dhimmis.⁶ But we will see. I hear there is a meeting with Christians tonight to inform them of their fate."

But not a single Christian attended the meeting. Fearing the worst, they stayed home. ISIS interpreted the no-show as a slap in the face, and as a result, there would be no more dialogue. The next morning, the Islamic State announced its verdict all over Mosul:

Christians, you have 24 hours to make your final decision. Because of the kindness of the new caliph, Abu Bakr
al-Baghdadi has declared that your options are as follows:
Convert to Islam, Pay the Jizya Tax, Leave, or Die. If you stay,
and do not receive our generous offer to convert to Islam, and
are unable to pay the protective tax, you will face the sword
immediately. The time for stalling will be over. You have until
noon tomorrow.[7]

That day, July 18, 2014, ISIS crews spread throughout Mosul
and painted the Arabic letter "N"—"of the Nazarene"—on
every Christian home in the city. On the morning of July 19,
forced evacuations began. More than 100,000 Christians threw
together the few belongings they could manage and exited
Mosul. Most possessions didn't make it out of town, though.
The State seized everything from wedding rings to baby diapers.

Medo, feigning enthusiasm for "the cause," gathered with
other ISIS soldiers outside the home of the Nimri family—all
Christians and all long-time friends of Medo's family.

"Medo, what are you doing here? I can't believe that you . . ."

Swallowing his shame, Medo signaled George Nimri, the
father, to stop talking.

"Please go while you can," Medo whispered to the man he
had loved since a child. "I will never forget you and your family.
And . . . pray for me."

He stepped quickly away from the Nimris and began
shouting again with ISIS men who were taunting Christians
scrambling to load their cars and get away. A half a block away,
he spied Faisal and was horrified as his friend beat a man who
tried to keep his young daughter from being taken away by an

ISIS leader. Faisal, Medo knew, was not simply playacting a role. He relished this newfound authority and poured himself into his new identity as an ISIS soldier.

Shrieks from a group of people exploded behind Medo, and as he whirled toward the uproar, he spotted a two-year-old boy, lying on the ground, frozen in fear, his eyes catatonic. A man in black stood over him, holding the muzzle of a semiautomatic rifle against the child's forehead.

The man barked at a weeping woman on her knees several feet away. "Will you let your son join the Islamic State now, or shall I blow his head off?"

A handful of savages circled the boy and guffawed at the mother and child. Neighborhood families standing outside the circle closed their eyes and shouted prayers skyward.

Suddenly alert to another disturbance, the man brandishing the weapon pulled the gun from the boy's head and pointed it in the direction of Faisal and the soldiers down the street. More young girls were being dragged away from crying families. The circle of lust-driven jihadists unraveled, and the men rushed toward the young females, intent on grabbing their share of the spoils. The mother lunged for her son, scooped him off the ground, and ran into the arms of the Christians who had prayed for a miraculous deliverance.

After eviscerating the Christian population of Mosul, the new government took on the eradication of any connection in the city to its twenty-century history of Christianity. After destroying all forty-five churches in Mosul, the terrorist army blew up the city's arguably most important biblical landmark.

ISIS bomb specialists rigged explosives in the 2,700-year-old tomb of the Old Testament prophet to the Ninevites, Jonah, and obliterated the ancient site. The detonation was their exclamation point at the conclusion of the drive to rid the city of its Christian population. The headline-grabbing terrorist army offered this statement to the world: the Islamic State is declaring war on history.

The knots in Medo's stomach had become chronic. Days after the initial Christian exodus, he hoped the worst was over. But he had not yet seen the fate of the few Jesus followers who chose to stay. Trying to collect his thoughts on a walk by himself the week after the evacuation, he turned from a side street onto a main thoroughfare. What he saw made him retch. Four men about his age, nails driven through their arms and legs, hung on crosses about fifty yards away. A pair of ISIS soldiers, left by their leaders to attend the crucifixion site, stood a stone's throw from the crosses.

Medo wanted badly to help these Christian men who had been made an example of the cost of remaining in Mosul. He felt strangely drawn to the suffering men and walked silently in their direction. From the now nearly deserted street, Medo judged that they had been there for several hours and certainly could not survive much longer in the scorching heat.

About thirty feet from the crosses, Medo stopped and stared at the bloody men. They were *praying and singing*. Medo could just barely make out the words, but what he heard was even more astounding than the crucifixions themselves. One asked God to forgive the ISIS soldiers. The others, voices barely above a whisper, sang a praise song: "*Zeedo el-Maseeh tasbeeh* . . . Praise Jesus Christ more and more."

One man's head hung awkwardly, but when he raised it up to take a breath, he smiled at Medo. Medo could see that the four men were at peace. But he felt like killing himself.

As he stood in front of the four crosses that day, something changed in Medo. Overwhelmed by despair, he had observed the dauntless Christians for many long minutes—perhaps even an hour; Medo wasn't sure how long. Listening to the final gasps of the man who had smiled at him, a jolt of courage ignited his own heart, and the reluctant terrorist knew he would abandon ISIS—and Mosul, if need be—the first chance he got. He had never felt more ashamed to be part of something.

He wasn't sure if the men were dead yet, but with his decision made, Medo turned his back on them and headed home, questions swirling in his brain. *Who are these people? My group is killing, kidnapping, raping, and torturing them. Yet this man smiled at me. Why? God help him and be merciful to him. Will I be able to get away? No matter. Even if I die, it will be better than taking part in this hideous world.*

For the next three months, Medo studied his options for escape. But once he was out of Mosul, who would want him? On the outside, known members of the Islamic State were killed on the spot, no questions asked.

Finally, the skeleton of an escape plan forming in his mind, Medo talked late one night with Faisal about options of a different sort.

"Faisal, where are we going now that all Christians and Yazidis are miles from Mosul?"

The two men lounged in the living room of a house that

once belonged to a Christian family. To help ease Medo's guilt when they commandeered the home, Medo had painted over the Arabic N on the front of the house. Although he hadn't known the family whose home was now property of the Islamic State, it reminded him of the Nimris.

"Do you think we will head south to fight the Shiite government soldiers or east to fight the Peshmerga?"[8]

Faisal puffed with pride and offered his assessment.

"If we go south, we risk the possibility of the Iranian army flooding Iraq with waves of fighters. But if we go east, someone will back the Peshmerga for sure—maybe the EU." He smirked. "Can you believe America is only dropping bombs? No US troops have shown up—even after their president was called out over some of the beheadings.

"I think it doesn't matter which way we go, Medo. We are doing Allah's business, and he gives us victory after victory. The fall of Mosul is proof enough. The Iraqi Army fielded 30,000 soldiers against our 1,500. Yet the pathetic cowards ran like little girls. Now the Islamic State has more than a billion dollars' worth of oil! Don't you see Allah's hand of blessing on us, my friend? Nothing will stop us now!"

Faisal laughed, the evil tone conjuring for Medo the revolting howl of terrorists hovering over the two-year-old boy with a rifle to his head. The pall over Faisal was nearly tangible, and Medo felt sick to his stomach. He could see in Faisal's eyes that his best friend had lost his soul to the Islamic State.

So that night, Medo made a run for it. He headed toward Dahuk, the capital of the Kurdish Governorate seventy-five miles north on Route 2. Halfway between the outskirts of Mosul and the turnoff to ancient Nineveh, Medo pulled a change of clothes out of the bag he had been carrying. About fifty yards off the road, he dug a shallow hole and buried his Islamic State uniform. The civilian clothes he had taken from the Christian home might cause him problems at an ISIS checkpoint, but he had time to plan for that.

For two days, Medo kept a safe distance between him and the main road as he made his way north. He prayed that Allah would protect him, especially at night when the Islamic State patrols roamed the area.

At the road to the Mosul Dam—once known as Saddam Dam—Medo crossed east over the highway toward Alqōsh and the Bayhidhra mountains. Even though Iraqi forces had taken the dam back from ISIS, the area was the site of ongoing attacks and should be avoided.

The thought of going to the Christian village of Alqōsh lifted Medo's spirits. Surely in the town where the prophet Nahum is buried, he would find a good-hearted family to take him in.

"Mr. Medo, I have a friend in the Peshmerga leadership, and he can help you get where you want to go." Michael Isaac not only took Medo into his home but offered to help him get to Turkey.

After one night in the Isaac household, Michael escorted Medo to a security office in the Alqōsh Airport, and an hour later, the former ISIS fighter boarded a plane for the thousand-mile flight to Istanbul.

The Turkish capital, though, offered no immediate solution to Medo's problem of where he belonged. For the better part of a week, Medo walked the streets of downtown Istanbul, processing thoughts about the cold-blooded brutality he had witnessed during the previous six months. When horrific flashbacks seized his mind, he stopped walking and sat wherever he could. While wandering Istanbul, he heard again the screams of young girls dragged from their parents, helpless to elude their fate as ISIS sex slaves. He thought of the thousands of Christians from whom the Islamic State took everything, gloating as the devastated families left the city with nothing. He replayed each murder—most horribly, the crucifixions he felt sure he would never forget.

Homeless in Istanbul, Medo wondered about his family. Were his parents alive? Had his sisters become "brides" of Islamic State killers? He wondered if Faisal was alive. He mourned his city and his friend, and he walked and walked. ISIS had destroyed his life.

Each day after sundown Medo drifted back to the Yazar Hotel, a more immediate concern on his mind: How long could he make the money from Michael Isaac last? The gift had been generous, but he must make the most of it.

At night, he lay in bed, staring at darkness as he pondered why the Christians of Mosul had behaved with such honor while losing everything: family members killed, women raped, boys and young men kidnapped. Yet, Mr. Isaac had opened his home even after Medo told him about escaping from the Islamic State military. And every night without fail, he pictured the Christian men on crosses praying for their killers . . . and singing . . . and smiling.

A week into his stay at the Yazar, Medo sat alone in the hotel's small lobby, ignoring the news report playing on the wall-mounted television.

"Hey, are you from Iraq?"

Medo startled at the voice and looked up to see an Iraqi man standing a few feet away.

"You look shell-shocked. Can you believe how our country is falling apart? The Islamic State needs to go down, man! If they get full control, our country is doomed!" He extended his hand. "I'm Sameer Dawoud—and you are?"

Sameer wore a friendly smile. Medo summoned one in return.

"I'm Medo Nasrallah. It's nice to meet another Iraqi."

The man pulled a chair close to Medo's and sat down. "If you don't mind my saying so, you look to be in bad shape, brother. Why don't you come with me tonight? I'm guessing you could use a friend or two, and I'm meeting with a few other Iraqis, then grabbing dinner at a restaurant on the Bosphorus River. Join me?"

Before the afternoon was out, Medo stood with Sameer on the sidewalk outside a white building in the northern section of the Istanbul peninsula.

"Is this what I think it is, Sameer? Is this a church?"

Sameer sensed his new friend backpedaling and put his arm around Medo. "My mistake, Medo. I didn't even ask if you are Christian or Muslim."

"I'm a Muslim, Sameer."

"Well, in this place, bro, it doesn't matter. Christians and Muslims are both welcome. Please stay for at least ten minutes, and if you feel weird after that, you can take off. Okay?" Sameer raised his eyebrows. "But I think you're going to like it."

Sameer held open the door to the meeting room, but as Medo stepped inside, he stopped as if paralyzed. For several seconds, he simply stared at the group gathered in the room. He glanced at Sameer, then raised his hands to cover his face and began to sob.

"Medo! Are you all right?" Sameer wrapped both arms around Medo and hugged him warmly. "Why are you crying, my friend?"

"I know this song they are singing." Medo choked out the words. "I've heard it before."

Zeedo el-Maseeh tasbeeh . . . Praise Jesus Christ more and more.

A WORD FROM MEDO

My heart melted when I again heard that hymn of praise the men on the crosses had been singing. The believers in Istanbul were so alive, and they sang with the same deep-seated joy as the crucified men in Mosul. Their peace didn't depend on the circumstances around them.

After two weeks in Istanbul, I gave my life to Jesus. The lives of these people convinced me that Jesus is the way to God. Sameer followed up the worship experience by giving me a Bible, and I devoured the New Testament, cleansing my mind with the very words of God. Images of life and hope replaced my mental images of death and misery.

More than ever, I now know the Islamic State is a tool of the devil. Unleashed by Satan himself, enemies of the cross continue to use ISIS in an unending assault on Christians and "the wrong" Muslims in my country of Iraq. There seems to be no end in sight to the unspeakable acts of terror.

As for me, once I gave my life to Jesus, my family disowned me and cut off all communication. By leaving Islam, I disgraced them, even though, privately, they despise the Islamic State as much as I do. Still living in Mosul, they fear their views might somehow be exposed. The Islamic State says people who think like my parents are not real Muslims. ISIS's vicious, divisive ways may well cause Islam itself to implode someday. I do not believe their methods are sustainable.

I found out a few months into my life in Istanbul that Faisal had been killed in a drone strike. If I had not escaped the Islamic State when I did, I would probably be dead too. My best friend was the first person I had thought about telling the good news to, but sadly, that will never happen.

So please pray for me. I've returned to Iraq and now live in Erbil in the Kurdistan region, less than a hundred miles from Mosul. Jesus gives me life, and I want nothing more than to tell others of how He saved me—a former member of ISIS, the most feared terrorist group in the world.

I came back to Iraq, and many think I am foolish. But I know that I am called to be a light in the darkness that covers my country. Let me ask you this: Where is Jesus calling you to be a light for Him?

Most Christians from Mosul fled to Erbil, so I have good fellowship here. I have asked many for forgiveness, and they often find it hard to believe that someone from ISIS actually loves Jesus. Frankly, it's hard for me to believe it at times, but Jesus is everyone's answer to the ethnic and religious hatred in the world.

The Islamic State spray-painted "N" on Christian homes in Mosul to mark them as "of the Nazarene" with disdain. When I arrived in Erbil, I found the Christian refugees that I helped expel from Mosul living in tents provided by the UN. What shocked me is that many of the refugees spray-painted "N" on their tents!

Because of their abiding hope in Jesus, the Islamic State did not defeat the Christians of Mosul. The Arabic "N" is now known around the world as a symbol for Christians who are not afraid to declare their love and loyalty to Jesus the Nazarene. My tent now has "N" on it. I was humbled and had tears in my eyes as I marked my new home.

At last, I no longer hate the people of ISIS either. I feel deeply sorry for them because of the deception that has ruined their lives. I ought to know, because I'm a former member of the Islamic State, and I worship Jesus with my new family.

Together we are Christians from Mosul.

7 THE SECRET POLICE SECRET

I hate you.

Mohammad Hajj hoped the man standing in the doorway of his apartment could read that thought in his eyes. *I would kill you if I could. All Christians like you deserve to die and go on to the hell waiting for you.* Mohammad's fellow-refugee neighbors had warned him about Rami Mousa. They said he would be around soon.

The man who introduced himself as Rami stepped back from the door as Mohammad loomed behind his quiet wife. The large man wearing a white dishdasha and black taqiyah[1] saw the flash of fear in his unwelcome visitor's eyes. Years of police work in Syria had honed the bearded man's ability to sense any hint of fright in those he confronted.

The infidel at the door mumbled a few words about welcoming them to Jordan and handed Manara Hajj two bags of groceries. Mohammad reached over his wife's shoulder, grabbed the tarp they used as a door, and slapped it across the opening. Clutching the groceries in her arms, Manara listened to Rami's footsteps fade as he descended the concrete stairway outside their apartment.

An hour later, Rami sat again in the safety of his own kitchen, thankful for the company of his wife.

"He would have killed me if he could." Staring into a cup of tea on the table in front of him, Rami shook his head. "I think if he had had a weapon today, I would be dead."

He looked up at his wife. "Someone told Mohammad I was one of the Bible people, and nothing else mattered to him—not even that I brought food for his family."

Rami Mousa had ministered to Syrian refugees for five years in northern Jordan and was used to bad days among displaced Muslims, but few people had unnerved him like Mohammad.

"Even before his wife opened the door, I felt the evil. Then he stared right into my soul and saw my fear. I froze, Sarah. And you know how I use scripture at times like that? I couldn't remember a single verse. After he shut the door in my face, the scripture I wanted came to me—'greater is He who is in you than he that is in the world.'

"When I was looking for his apartment, one of Hajj's neighbors told me he had been in the secret police before he fled Damascus." Rami lifted the teacup to his lips. "I hope I never see Mohammad Hajj again."

Rami and his wife sat in silence for several minutes, sipping tea, before Rami spoke again. "Sarah, I've been thinking and praying this past month. I'm not sure we should do this anymore." Rami sighed. "Work with the refugees, I mean. Every single day we hear another story that rips my heart out. I know it does yours too. And the nightmares they give me feel purely demonic." Rami paused. His eyes drifted to Sarah's silky black hair. "You see how little I eat at dinner each night. What I hear during the day ruins my appetite. I must have some form of post-traumatic stress disorder."

Sarah placed her right hand on the table and slid it toward her husband's. "Rami, my love, we can first of all thank God that we live in Jordan and that we are not trying to raise little John in Syria. God forbid that a war like theirs ever spills over the border. I heard the other day that ninety-two bombs exploded in Damascus alone. How do people survive there?"

Sarah nodded toward the child playing quietly on the floor beside them. "By the way, little John looked out the window several times today, wondering where his daddy was."

Rami lifted the one-year-old boy onto his lap and tickled him firmly. The boy squealed. Named after the apostle John, Rami's son had his mother's sparkling brown eyes and his father's endless energy. Rami released the laughing child, and John wobbled down the hall, a clear signal that the little boy was ready to play his nightly game of hide-and-go-seek with his adoring Abu[2] John.

"How long have you been friends with Mohammad Hajj?"

Salim Mashni politely but firmly stopped Rami the next morning as the minister to refugees stepped out of his apartment building. The forty-ish Jordanian General Intelligence agent stood just outside Rami's kitchen window, the contrast of his smartly dry-cleaned black suit and the red and white kafiyah on his head making him look taller than his five-foot-ten-inch frame. Mashni held a fist full of notes, and a cigarette clung to his bottom lip as he stared blankly at Rami, waiting for an answer.

With this flood of refugees into Jordan across the northern border, now it seems that our secret police are standing on every corner in Irbid. Rami let his irritation subside before answering the determined interrogator.

"He's *not* my friend. I only met him yesterday. He's just another refugee from Syria—and a mean one at that!"

Salim Mashni checked an item off his list of notes.

"Did he tell you about his work in Syria or mention anything concerning what he did there?"

"No. In fact, he never said a word to me. His wife was nice, but he just stared me down. One of his neighbors told me that Mohammad had been in the Syrian secret police. I'm not sure why he would leave such a position. It's about the only spot left in Bashar Al-Assad's government with any job security these days."

Salim Mashni ignored the quip and shifted on his feet. Pinching the cigarette between the thumb and two fingers of his left hand, he pulled it from his lips and tilted his head in Rami's direction. "That's exactly what we want to find out, Rami. We think it's strange that he left too." He leaned his head back and looked down his nose at Rami. "We want you to go back and visit him again. It's a matter of national security. One of the reasons our Hashemite Kingdom is strong and secure is that citizens like you, Rami, help us by being listening ears."

Rami, the informant. He wasn't sure he liked the thought. "What do you want to know about Hajj?"

"Many things. Is he still working for Assad? Has he come here to uncover ISIS cells forming in Jordan? With the continual drone strikes, it certainly would be easier for ISIS to organize new recruits here in Jordan than in Syria." Mashni paused and scanned his list before continuing.

"Has he defected and joined ISIS? How could a practicing Sunni Muslim work for Assad anymore? That seems odd to me. Is he on the run for being a deserter?"

"Mr. Mashni," Rami interrupted—he had a few questions of his own. "Why don't you ask him those questions yourself? Why do you want me to help?"

Interrogating an officer in the secret police was uncharted territory. *They* ask the questions. Yet here he was, questioning a Jordanian secret policeman about a Syrian secret policeman.

By the time the conversation ended, the man from General Intelligence had piqued Rami's curiosity. Perhaps he wouldn't mind seeing Mohammad Hajj again after all. Discovering the whole story about the sinister refugee from Syria could be interesting.

Three months before fleeing to Jordan, the thirty-five-year-old Syrian secret policeman faced the most difficult decision of his life. Either of Mohammad Hajj's choices would likely cost him his life. No matter, though, Mohammad knew he could no longer serve under President Bashar Al-Assad now that the cruelty of his administration had finally come so close. His good friend and cousin Hassan Rashid did not deserve to die.

Hassan's merciless death changed forever Mohammad's estimation of Syria's "beloved" president. A respectable Sunni banker in Tartous, Hassan preferred Assad's rule to the alternatives, but because he "knew some people" the Alawite government feared might be connected with ISIS, Assad's people considered him a high-risk individual. The result for Hassan Rashid was a body shredded by a variety of inhumane, uniquely Assad-style tortures before being decapitated in front of his wife and children.

In deciding how to abandon his post at the Mukhabarat,[3] Mohammad thought he had only two options: run away or join ISIS to retaliate. But since Mohammad would never run, that left him with only one choice—until he discovered that several trusted friends hated Assad as much as he did.

"What are really the odds that we could assassinate Bashar Al-Assad?" Mohammad eyed each of the three men seated on the floor of a dimly lit basement on the outskirts of Aleppo. He shook his head. "We may be insiders, but you know as well as I do that even we can't get close enough to kill him. No one can. Only his family and the *inner circle* are allowed anywhere near the president." He was stating the obvious to the three other veteran Mukhabarat agents.

"His so-called public appearances are all staged with government people desperately trying to look like average citizens." He paused as the other three men nodded in concert. "But there are other ways to bring him down."

None of the men in the room had yet cut their ties to jobs, which offered one last hope to avenge the deaths of people they had cherished. Their work provided the necessary cover, and if all went as planned, the charade they were living would soon be over. Then, if Assad didn't yet know by name these men who had worked so faithfully for him, he—and all of Syria—would soon know who they were.

"I've been thinking about this since Hassan Rashid's death," Mohammad continued. "We may not be able to bring down President Assad ourselves, but we can get the international media to do it for us. And the immense fringe benefit to all four of us is that we won't have to join ISIS to accomplish my plan. Once the world news displays what Assad is doing to the Syrian people, dozens of countries will line up to get rid of him. All we have to do is deliver video proof of Assad's stockpile of chemical weapons. We know he has used chlorine, saran, and mustard gas. Each of us has seen it ourselves! Most of the world already knows it, too, but we can provide evidence that outsiders can no longer deny or turn away from.

"*We* are the key." Mohammad swept his index finger in a circle at the three men listening to him. "If four secret police who worked for the president risk their lives to tell the whole story about Assad's pitiless use of chemical weapons on his own people and show undeniable evidence, how could he continue in power? World leaders will collectively rise up and remove Assad if we show them how many dirty weapons he has and how freely he uses them. We just have to find the stockpiles. I believe they are just south of here or perhaps at the cache west of Damascus. To do this, we won't even have to fire a single bullet."

"Of course not. All the bullets will be used firing at *us!*" Hakeem Barzani spat the words and stood abruptly. "We'd never live past the day we record the video. How would we even get near the stockpile, let alone get video footage of it? Your plan won't ever be more than a dream. Don't you realize every other disillusioned government official has probably thought of doing the same thing? I'm out! This is insane."

"No, it's not!"

The four men turned toward a new voice. Omar Najjar entered the room, and Mohammad and the two men still seated jumped to their feet.

"Omar! We thought you were dead." Mohammad gaped at the Syrian military hero standing by the basement door.

"Everyone did." Omar Najjar smirked. "That's the government's favorite story when yet another Syrian officer defects from Mr. Assad's army. It's an epidemic now."

Najjar stepped toward the circle of men. "I'm alive, and, Mohammad, I like your plan. That's why I'm here. I heard about Hassan's death and knew you would not sit back and do nothing. It's not in any of us, I hope . . . ," he smiled at Hakeem Barzani, "to continue blindly following the madman of Syria." Barzani grimaced and looked at the floor.

"The reason this plan could work is because all five of us served Assad for years. People will believe us." Najjar shook a triumphal fist toward his companions. "We can get to the stockpile. I know two of the guards, and like many others, it seems they may be more than ready to change sides."

Mohammad's eyes widened. "You know where the chemical weapons are hidden?"

Omar smiled and spoke slowly. "I know where they are. Yes, I do. I also know where President Assad is producing more chemical weapons *right now*, here in Syria."

Mohammad mouthed the word "Wow" and stared for several seconds past Omar's shoulder at the concrete wall. The three friends stood silent, mouths open.

After discussing their next steps and avowing the secrecy needed, the five men exited the basement, one at a time, for the next hour.

"Manara, tomorrow I go on a covert mission."

Mohammad's twenty-three-year-old wife looked up at her

husband, a partially filled plate of scrambled eggs, tomatoes, and fava beans suspended in her hand over the stove.

"I could be killed." The dark-haired woman dropped Mohammad's favorite breakfast on the hot surface.

"What are you talking about, Mohammad? Why would you be involved in a covert mission? You're secret police! You *uncover* covert missions, not go on them!" The desperate woman ignored the spilled food smoldering on the stove and glared at her husband.

"Not anymore." Mohammad spoke softly, then looked down at his cup of Turkish coffee. Without raising his eyes, he continued quietly but firmly. "After Hassan's needless, gruesome death at the hands of the president's goons, I could no longer take it. Manara, I have closed my eyes to too many things over the years. The cruel, unjust treatment of our Sunni people has torn my heart out over time. I hoped that Assad might be the one person who could hold this fractured country together."

He looked up at his wife. "That's why I stayed. That's why I kept working for him. Who else would lead us? ISIS? Jabhat al-Nusra? Ha! They kill their own people!" He raised the cup to his lips and sipped coffee. "Ever since Hassan died, though, I've been merely collecting a paycheck and waiting—waiting for the right time to retaliate and bring Assad down for good."

Passion flashed in Mohammad's eyes. He raised his voice, nearly shouting. "I've changed, Manara. I would join ISIS *now* if I could get revenge for my cousin's death!"

Manara stepped back from the stove and away from her husband's outburst. "Mohammad, lower your voice. The neighbors might hear . . . for all we know, our home might even be bugged."

Mohammad sneered. "It probably is bugged. I wouldn't put it past that paranoid maniac. Remember my words, Manara. President Assad will go down. He will pay for what he did to Hassan."

Manara startled as Mohammad gripped her left arm and led her firmly into the bathroom. He loosened his grasp and stroked her hand soothingly. Then he whispered, "Tomorrow is the day, Manara. Which means you must go too. Pack a small bag for each of the children. You'll have to leave here very early. I've already arranged for a car to come for you at 4 A.M. By midmorning, you and the children will be at the Jordanian border. A friend will be waiting to take you across. You'll have no problems, and you'll be safe there. If all goes well, I'll call you by dinner tomorrow night."

"But, Mohammad, who am I meeting?" Manara could barely control her panic. "What are their names? How will I know them?"

"It's best that you don't know the names. That way, you won't be covering anything up if you're questioned. I've arranged for you to travel on back roads and go through as few checkpoints as possible. When the border guards ask where you're going and why, just tell them you're a refugee. By then, I'll be safely hiding, Allah willing."

"A refugee? Oh, Mohammad, no!"

Mohammad placed his lips gently on his wife's and kissed her for several seconds. "I'm sorry, Manara, but I must leave now. I'm heading to the Damascus area. I love you, and if my plan works, we'll be together again in Jordan. Kiss the children and tell them I hope to see them." Mohammad blinked hard. "Tell them that I *will see them* soon after Daddy's out-of-town business is finished."

Still holding Manara's hand, Mohammad led her out of the

bathroom and back to the kitchen. He released her, walked to the back door, and turned in her direction.

"Good-bye, habibti."

Less than twenty-four hours later, in the shadowy dining room of an abandoned house just outside of Damascus, five conspirators reviewed their plan to topple President Bashar Al-Assad of Syria.

"We'll be in and out in fifteen minutes with the video in our hands." Omar Najjar spoke confidently. "I have the phone numbers of BBC correspondents to call as soon as we are safely away from the site. First, though, the video must hit the Internet just in case we're killed before I can place the calls. Facebook, Twitter, and YouTube will launch the video, and the BBC will legitimize it. By the time Bashar Al-Assad is having breakfast, we'll be in Jordan."

Mohammad added details he and Omar had formulated during the night. "You may be asking yourself: 'Who is going to roll over so we can get to the chemical stash?' Well, you can take your pick! If Assad knew how many of his soldiers are willing to turn the other way for a price, he'd be on a plane to Moscow already. We also have another big factor in our favor." Mohammad gestured at the Syrian war hero sitting beside him.

"Omar's reputation preceded him. The two people he called were as surprised as we were to find out he is alive, and his friends are more than willing to help. They owed him one—lots of people do. We didn't have to pay them anything.

"The guard at the gate and one at the underground warehouse will be going with us. Their families have already left the country."

The Syrian military officer and the secret police agent relished the final moments of detailing their plan and giving each man their assignment. Mohammad glanced at his watch: 3:15—about three hours till sunrise.

Omar stood slowly, looking each man in the eye. "The point of no return is here. Gentlemen, it's time for the world to see what it's like to live in Syria. These weapons were surely used in the Zamalka attack.[4] And I believe nerve gas is now being stored for use in Assad's "scorched earth" last resort if it comes to that. More than five hundred people have died in Assad's chemical attacks, and so far, the world does nothing but watch. This time, though, the BBC report will be different. No one on the outside will any longer have plausible deniability." Omar paused, drawing in a deep breath. "Now, let's go, and as we do, keep this in your mind at all times today: *Bashar Al-Assad must die!*"

Mohammad nodded solemnly and signaled their audience to follow. Omar Najjar walked behind the quartet and out the back door where a GAZ Tigr 4x4 jeep-truck awaited them. The dull green Russian-made troop mover looked no different than dozens of similar vehicles they would pass on their way to and into the Syrian government installation targeted for their mission. Entering the warehouse complex would not alarm a soul.

Omar turned in the driver's seat of the GAZ and pulled a pile of Syrian army uniforms from the utility shelves behind him.

"Another favor for Omar?" Hakeem smiled as he unfolded a uniform.

Omar patted his own chest, nodded, grinned back at Hakeem. Then he turned and shifted the truck into gear. With a loud clank, the transport lurched forward.

Less than five minutes later, occupants of the troop transport stared silently out the vehicle's diminutive windows at the lights shimmering in the opulent Assad family palace overlooking Damascus, just west of the ancient city.

"Bashar Assad has the dirty bombs as close to his palace as possible. Since other parts of the country are so unstable, he keeps a close eye on them." Omar sounded like a guide describing the scenery for a busload of tourists. "It's dangerous to keep them here, of course, but who knows where the Assads really are on any given day? Asma and the children are probably out of the country anyway."

The GAZ rolled to a stop at the first security check, and a guard appeared by Omar's window. "Everything is in order here. I will see you soon, Omar."

The vehicle accelerated slowly and drove casually into the compound. It pulled within thirty feet of a small building Omar had explained was the cover for a vast underground warehouse. Intending to leave the truck's engine running, Omar set the parking brake, but before he and Mohammad could open the front doors, gunfire cracked outside and the five men in the GAZ heard the clatter of bullets against the truck's armored plates.

"Ambush!" Mohammad hollered and ducked below the dashboard as a dozen Syrian soldiers raced from the building, weapons blazing. Omar gunned the engine, bent low in his seat, and accelerated toward three soldiers, forcing them to stop firing and dive away from the oncoming vehicle.

The windshield shattered in a rain of lead as Omar spun the truck in a U-turn. A drumroll of bullets rattled the sides of the GAZ and eliminated the remaining windows. Omar sped toward the gate but shifted into neutral as the truck rolled toward the security point. Hakeem cracked open the back door, and the guard who had ushered them into the compound dove in. Unhurt but panicked, the guard lay on his stomach and covered his head with his arms. Hakeem rocked back in his seat as Omar gunned the engine. Regaining balance, he reached for the door and pulled it shut.

Omar cursed for several minutes as the GAZ careened around the eastern edge of Damascus. Finally, he shouted, "Bashar Al-Assad still survives!" His eyes flared. "But one day . . . one day." Omar shook his head.

Air blasting through what was once the windshield roared in their ears as the six men rode without talking. South of Damascus, the truck sped for several miles along Highway M5, still relatively deserted in the predawn light, then turned east on a nondescript side road. Omar slowed the truck to avoid any more attention than necessary for a windowless, pock-marked GAZ. Keeping his eyes on the road, he cocked his head to speak to the five other men.

"Off the highway, it will be easier to disappear, but it's going to be a rough ride to the border. I know back roads through the Druze villages that will keep us out of sight. Once we're near the Daraa crossing, we'll ditch the truck, split up, and hike across the border." He paused, energy draining from his voice. "I should have known someone would talk."

Three months after the failed attempt to expose Assad's chemical weapons, Mohammad Hajj peeked through a hole in the tarp serving as front door of the shabby apartment he and Manara now called "home." His stomach knotted and he sneered as he recognized the obviously nervous man standing outside. It was Rami Mousa. The hate welled again in Mohammad.

Manara slid her arm past Mohammad and flipped back the tarp.

"Donations have been plentiful, so there's an extra chicken this week." Rami forced a smile.

Manara squeezed in front of Mohammad, who stood statue-like, his eyes daring Rami to be kind. The woman scowled at her obstinate husband, then turned, smiling, toward Rami.

"Shukron,[5] Rami! Thank you for feeding our family. I never would have guessed we could gain weight as refugees! We are all thankful, aren't we Mohammad?"

Mohammad ignored his wife, but Manara continued, cheerful. "Maybe I can meet your wife next time."

Weak smile still in place, Rami nodded slowly. "Yes. That would be nice."

The partially welcome visitor handed over a chicken and assorted groceries. "I hope to see you again," he said without conviction.

Later that afternoon, Rami and Sarah drank Lipton tea at their kitchen table while Rami again sorted his disturbed feelings about Mohammad Hajj. Sarah pushed a plate of her husband's favorite sweets across the table. Little John, asleep on his father's lap, stirred as Rami pulled two Snickers bars off the plate and onto the table.

"He's got to be demon-possessed, Sarah. His eyes blaze with hate like I've never seen." Rami stripped the paper off a Snickers bar. "But I'm not going to let the enemy frighten me. *Satan* is my enemy, not Mohammad, and this time when I saw him was certainly awkward, but I felt the presence of the Lord all around me." He bit into the candy and looked thoughtfully at his wife. "I pity him, Sarah . . . I really do. In fact, will you pray with me for him?"

Sarah nodded. "Of course."

Rami reached for his wife's hand. "Jesus, we pray for Mohammad. We pray for Manara who has to put up with him! For some reason, you brought them into our lives, and we know there is nothing too hard for you, Lord. Please help us help them."

The next morning, the buzz of Rami's cell phone startled Sarah, Rami, and John, who was sleeping between them. Rami checked the time as he picked up the phone: 6:00. He barely said hello before the man on the phone nearly shouted at him.

"Rami! This is Mohammad Hajj. You brought us food yesterday. Do you remember me?"

"Actually I do remember you, Mohammad." Rami raised his eyebrows and cut his eyes at Sarah. She frowned and mouthed the question, "Mohammad?"

"Rami, Manara fell down the stairs yesterday evening and broke her leg terribly. She's in severe pain and has been crying all night. We have no money, and I'm not a legal refugee. I don't know what to do. Rami, you're the only friend I have."

Rami dropped out of bed and sat on the floor in shock. Had he really just heard Mohammad say he was his friend?

Sarah grabbed John and slipped onto the floor next to her husband. Rami's next words shocked *her*.

"I'll be there as soon as I can."

Rami clicked off the phone and turned to Sarah. "I have to go to the hospital. Mohammad needs me."

"Mohammad Hajj?" Sarah had to ask, just to confirm the source of their stunning wake-up call.

"Yes! His wife is hurt, and he needs my help." He looked at Sarah in disbelief "He said I'm his only friend!" Rami laughed. "If that's how he treats a friend, I'd hate to be his enemy." Rami pulled his wife and prayer partner close and kissed her on the forehead.

"The surgery will cost $1,500."

The front desk nurse at King Abdullah University Hospital in Irbid wouldn't budge. Rami had presented his best arguments as to why the amount was unreasonably high, but the immovable woman wasn't selling souvenirs to a tourist. The hospital price was firm.

Without further haggling, Rami paid that morning's emergency room bill and breathed a silent prayer for the much larger sum needed to cover Manara's surgery the next day. He walked across the lobby and sat down next to the desperate couple. Tears rolled silently down Manara's cheeks, her head drooping toward the floor.

"Manara, don't worry." Rami decided the time had come to be transparent with his faith. "God has this one. He will provide. Sarah and I have been praying for both of you. In fact, we couldn't sleep last night. Even before you called, all we could think of was you and your family."

Rami turned to Mohammad. "Let's get Manara back to your apartment. Sarah will bring over a bucket of ice and some Advil. But before we go, I've got a phone call to make."

As Rami reached for his phone, the keypad lit up. He recognized the number. *What a time for the secret police to call!*

"Yes, Mr. Mashni, what can I help you with?"

Salim Mashni cleared his smoker's throat and spoke firmly. "Rami, stay away from Mohammad Hajj. We have reason to believe he is part of a plot to launch a wave of terrorist attacks in Jordan. He may have been a secret policeman in Syria, but he is a full-fledged member of the Islamic State now." Mashni cleared his throat. "You were just seen with him at the hospital, so we have a few questions for you. I'll be visiting you tonight, Rami."

Knowing he could not refuse Salim Mashni's inquest, Rami politely agreed, and the call ended. As Mohammad rolled Manara toward the exit in a wheelchair, Rami dialed a phone number in the United States of America.

Mohammad folded himself into the backseat of Rami's 2001 Toyota Camry. With the front seat reclined nearly flat, Manara's head rested close to Mohammad. He leaned in and kissed her forehead.

Standing by the open front door, Rami finished his phone call, then dropped into the driver's seat. He flashed a smile at the passenger next to him.

"Manara, your surgery will be tomorrow morning as planned. I just got off the phone with my friend, Hanna. She leads a ministry in America that works with Muslim women. Hanna is a big-hearted woman of God, and she's having money for your surgery wired to my account right now. It won't cost you a single JD."[6]

"Does Hanna live in Detroit?" Manara asked softly. "I have heard Detroit has many Muslims. Does she work with women at a mosque there?"

Rami saw the confusion in Manara's eyes.

"I can't believe this," the injured woman continued. "Why would she help when she doesn't even know me?"

Rami prayed silently for the right way to answer Manara.

"No. Hanna doesn't live in Detroit, and she's not a Muslim either. She lives in Dallas, Texas." He paused, feeling almost as nervous as he had at the Hajj's front door the day before. "She . . . Hanna . . . follows Jesus."

Manara and Mohammad tried to comprehend the words. Rami looked from Manara to Mohammad as the couple sat in silence. Manara's voice drew his attention back to the woman in the front seat.

"Rami, would you please call her back?"

"Yes, I can do that, but why?"

"I would like you to thank her for me." Manara glanced at Mohammad, then back at Rami. "Please thank my new American friend."

Manara covered her face with her hands and sobbed, but not from the pain in her broken leg.

"Another cup of tea, Mr. Mashni?"

The representative of the Jordanian secret police glanced at Sarah Mousa, forcing himself not to stare at the stunning woman in a scarlet, floor-length Bedouin-style dress as she hovered near his chair in the Mousa living room.

"Yes, please." Mashni cleared his throat. "And I'll take some more of those sweets." He planned to stay awhile.

Bored with Mashni's presence, Rami had tired of answering the same questions multiple times. He suspected that his interviewer was looking for inconsistencies in his story. *Fortunately, there is no variation in the facts when a person is telling the truth and has nothing to hide.* Rami tried not to let his irritation show.

"I really don't think Mohammad Hajj is a threat to the

Jordanian government, Mr. Mashni. I used to think so, but I don't anymore." Rami hoped his confident statement would satisfy Salim Mashni, and the man would simply leave.

"We'll see about that." Rami's endorsement of Mohammad Hajj did not impress the man from the secret police. He finished a second plate of candy and two more cups of tea. Finally, his car roared away from the Mousa residence a few minutes before midnight.

Two days after the evening-long examination by Salim Mashni and a day after Manara Hajj's surgery, Mohammad wheeled his wife into an examining room at the office of Dr. Abdul Aziz.

"I'm sorry to say there were complications with the surgery." The doctor spoke respectfully to the refugee couple. "I'm not sure it worked the way we had hoped." Dr. Aziz looked down at the floor. "In fact, her leg may be worse off now."

The surgeon let the news sink in. Mohammad and Manara studied the man for several seconds before he raised his eyes and spoke again.

"Manara, you need another surgery. This time by a specialist we do not have here at King Abdullah University. I will make arrangements at a private hospital that I know can do what you require." The doctor nodded politely and turned toward the door of the examining room, concluding the meeting.

As Dr. Aziz stepped out of the room, Hajj's phone rang.

"Mohammad!" Rami's excitement gushed out of the phone. "I just saw that the two of you aren't at your apartment. Those stairs are nasty, by the way. I'm on them right now, and I almost fell myself.

"The Lord placed you on my heart again, and I knew He was telling me to call you. Here's the message: Don't worry about the next surgery. God won't leave you hanging. The money will be on its way soon!"

Mohammad pressed the phone against his cheek, too dumbfounded to respond.

"Mohammad?"

"Rami, how did you know Manara is going to need another surgery? Did you talk to her doctor?" Mohammad placed his free hand on Manara's shoulder. "We just found out a few minutes ago."

Manara's questioning eyes looked up at her husband.

Rami caught his breath, then continued gingerly with a daring explanation. "No, I didn't talk to the doctor. But last night Sarah and I prayed for Manara, and . . . well . . . *Jesus told us.* That's how we know."

Mohammad just listened.

"Don't grab a taxi. I'm on my way to pick you up!"

Mohammad Hajj turned off the phone and sat against the examination table. He sighed deeply. "Manara, I've been a secret policeman in Syria for fifteen years. But Rami . . . It's like he has us wired and is following our every move. Everything he says and does is perfectly timed. I don't know how he does it."

The couple sat quietly for a minute. Then Mohammad opened the door and rolled Manara through the waiting room. As they reached the exit, Rami's Toyota pulled up to the front of the building.

Mohammad chuckled. "See what I mean, Manara? Here he is!"

Manara could walk again by the time Rami and Sarah welcomed a group of American missionaries to Jordan. At a get-acquainted breakfast for the team, the first story Rami told them was about the angry secret policeman from Syria.

"Most intimidating man I have ever met—and that says a lot since I live in Jordan! It's amazing how the Lord turned our relationship around; we're friends now. In fact, I told him you were coming, and he wants to meet you. Manara still walks with a slight limp, but she has no pain and should make a full recovery thanks to the second surgery. Mohammad wants to thank you in person for making the surgeries possible.

"But: Let's not talk to him about Jesus on this first visit. I tried that about two months ago, and the old Mohammad resurfaced. He glared at me like the first day we met. He's a dedicated Sunni Muslim, and he's just not ready. Maybe one day he will be—that's what I'm praying—but he's not now."

After breakfast and some training in local customs, Patrick, Lisa, and Rami jumped in the Toyota Camry. Minutes later, they climbed the concrete staircase that had caused Manara so much grief, navigating around the rebar protruding from the base of each step.

Patrick laughed. "This must be quite a role reversal for you, Rami! We're visiting a secret policeman in *his* home." He swept an arc with his hand. "If that's what you can call this place. It's just an unfinished—and abandoned!—building. Hardly an *apartment*. Not even any windows or doors. How pitiful."

The three visitors stepped, in turn, onto a dusty landing. Patrick and Lisa followed Rami to a grungy tarp hanging across a nearby doorway.

Manara pulled back the makeshift door and welcomed her American guests. Inside, Mohammad rose from the floor like a Bedouin sheik, slowly and with dignity.

Mohammad spoke first. "I want to thank you for what you did for Manara." He paused while Rami translated from Arabic to English for the guests. "Your generosity was unexpected, and I also thank Rami for contacting you." He nodded at their translator. "I've lived in Syria all my life, and Americans have always been . . . should I say . . . not the best of friends to our country."

"I know what you mean, Mohammad!" Rami translated Patrick's quick response. "What are the chances of a couple of Americans sitting with a Syrian family who escaped their country in the middle of the war? But we're the ones who were blessed by *you*. We prayed for you, and when we heard Manara was finally walking again, we felt like having a party.

"I can imagine this has been the hardest year of your life, and I'm sorry for all your family has gone through. Will you tell us your story of how you made it to Jordan? With three children, it must have been extremely dangerous to make a run for it."

Mohammad offered the visitors floor cushions, inviting them to sit with him, and for nearly an hour, he and Manara described the miseries and terror of living in Syria, ending with an account of Hassan Rashid's horrendous death. After the painful story, the group sensed it was time to change subjects.

"Lisa has a story for you." Patrick shifted on the floor and looked at his female companion.

Surprised, Rami guessed what was coming. Also caught off guard, Lisa stumbled into the story she had practiced with the team just that morning but had not planned to share.

"This is a true story from the Word of God—the Bible. One day, Jesus and His disciples were in a boat . . ."

She recounted the story of Jesus calming the sea, then asked Mohammad and Manara for their reaction.

"What did you two like about that story?"

Mohammad Hajj spoke thoughtfully, processing what Lisa had just told them. "Jesus knew the men with him were afraid and helpless in the storm. It reminds me of our story."

After a fifteen-minute discussion between Lisa and the Muslim couple, Patrick jumped in again. "Lisa has another story!"

Lisa chuckled softly. "This is another true story from God's Word. One day, Jesus was in a crowd, and a woman with an issue of blood touched the hem of His garment . . ."

Mohammad and Manara drank in Lisa's words.

"Mohammad, you and Manara really enjoy these stories, don't you?" Patrick thought the couple might leap off their cushions in excitement.

"Yes, Patrick, we do!'

Mohammad reached under his cushion, and when he drew his hand out, Rami gasped.

"We love these stories." Mohammad held up a green paperback New Testament. "Because we've been reading the Bible each night before we go to sleep.

"This was a gift we received at the medical clinic from a woman named Jen, about a month ago. She told me this was the most important book ever written. So we started reading that night."

"We told you God's stories, and you've been reading them too. But now let me tell you *my* story." Patrick raised his eyebrows and smiled excitedly. "I gave up religion years ago. I was a religious person, but I had to leave it behind—too many rules. I couldn't even remember all of them. I kept forgetting what I was supposed to do, and I would get in trouble with my *religion*.

"One day, I realized that in all my years of trying to keep the rules, I wasn't any closer to God. My heart was empty!"

Mohammad and Manara looked at each other, bewildered.

"Religion was a dead end for me. So I gave my life to Jesus and started following Him. That's when everything changed and life really began for me."

Mohammad Hajj smiled at Manara and grabbed her hand. She grinned back as her husband shouted in joy. "This is what we've been looking for our whole lives!" He closed his eyes and turned his face toward the ceiling. "It's Jesus, isn't it? He's the one we've been searching for! I knew it was Jesus!" He opened his eyes and peered at Lisa, then Patrick. "I've even had dreams about Him!"

Rami Mousa leaped to his feet and hollered back at his Syrian friend. "Yes, Mohammad! It's Jesus!"

A WORD FROM MOHAMMAD

I was a secret policeman in Syria; now I'm a secret believer in Jordan. But before meeting Rami, my life was all about getting revenge.

I wanted to kill Bashar Al-Assad more than anything. I served faithfully in the secret police for years, trying to break up any kind of uprising before it started, and I knew everything about everybody in my beloved city of Tartous. I even interrupted secret church meetings and routinely interrogated Christians.

One time I broke into an underground church having the Lord's Supper. Although I hated the Christians, I also pitied them since I thought they were going to hell someday. That's why I pitied—but hated—Rami. But I didn't hate anyone as much as I hated Assad.

How could I overlook our president's cruelty? As an Alawite, he treated my people—the Sunnis—with contempt and unspeakable brutality for years. And his reign doesn't even include what his father before him, Hafez al-Assad, did to my people. The killing of my closest friend Hassan pushed me over the edge.

I don't know where Omar, Hakeem, or the others ended up after our failed plan to topple Assad. And I don't know if the guard at the warehouse made it. I haven't seen any of them since we scrambled across the border to Jordan.

Of course, now I see that being in Jordan was part of God's plan for my life. So was Manara's accident. That's when I finally realized Rami helped us because he truly cared.

God continued to shock me daily. That the Christian Americans I had never met paid for not one but two surgeries? Unreal. In Syria, I never recall hearing one good story about Americans. "The Evil Empire" was all we heard from the government-controlled news.

Now all of my hate is gone. Jesus has given me a new heart. Even though I was a proud and angry secret policeman in Syria, now I'm a humble refugee like millions of others. But God had to do that to reach me. He has taken away my hatred and has forgiven me. I don't even hate Bashar Al-Assad anymore. I actually feel sorry for him and pray that he finds Jesus someday. I also pray for my people and ask God to end this miserable war. I pray the chemical weapons are destroyed before they can be used again.

Rami is discipling me now. I can never thank Sarah and him enough for their love and care. He is one of the bravest believers I know. He remains here, helping others, even though his life is in danger because he is so bold for Jesus. He has been questioned and threatened—and Salim Mashni watches him continually. He watches me too. How ironic! Now I am being watched by the secret police!

Manara and I have decided to give complete control of our lives over to our Savior, Jesus. Some of you have loved Jesus much longer than we, but have you taken this important step of laying down all your possessions and giving them over to Him?

Recently, Patrick brought his wife, Hanna, and her friend Ruth, along with Lisa to visit us. The three women of God sent the funds for Manara's surgeries, and we wanted to thank them in person. I asked Patrick a few questions.

"Jesus talks about giving, and I believe the word is 'tithing.' But we are Syrian refugees and not allowed to make any money here in Jordan. So can we give some of our clothes that we have been given to those who are in greater need? Also, when the refugee food packages are delivered to us, can we give some of our food away to other refugees who need it? Do you think this would be okay with Jesus?"

I was relieved to hear Patrick say that I had the true spirit of giving and that Jesus was pleased with this idea.

I don't know where we will eventually live or what God's plan is for us. As refugees we have few rights. But that is not my concern. I just want to be faithful where Jesus has planted me here in Jordan. I know I'm called to reach my Syrian people. How I ache for them to be set free! Even in the midst of a war—and the seemingly unquenchable fires of hatred—people can be free in Jesus.

If God opens the door for us to go back to our country, I will be a hunted man. Former secret police will be on the top of the list for the current secret police! But I long for Syrians to know that the answer to life is not found in Islam or any other religion. Manara and I along with our children gave up religion and all the rules. It doesn't satisfy a thirsty soul. And it doesn't fill an empty heart that is searching to be close to our Father. We now all know the answer.

It's Jesus, isn't it?

8 THE JERUSALEM PEACE PLAN

S ami Abbasi squinted through the railing of a first-story balcony in an abandoned building on Gaza City's Salah al-Din Road. The IDF[1] Jeep approached like a dog sniffing its environment, looking for trouble.

They are *dogs, and if they're looking for trouble, I'll give it to them*, he mused.

The thirteen-year-old Palestinian rolled a baseball-size rock in his right hand, estimating the distance to the approaching Israelis. To bolster his resolve, he counted to three and then heaved the stone. The missile scored a direct hit, smashing the windshield. Sami rewarded himself with a fist pump, launched his body over the railing to the ground several feet below, and dashed toward the outdoor market a block away. The injured vehicle stopped. A Jewish soldier in drab green erupted from the passenger side and sprinted after the boy.

Game on! Sami zigzagged through the maze of shops, laughing as he left his pursuer struggling through the chaos of vendors. He knew the chase would be short-lived. Not only was it nearly impossible to track someone through the twists and turns of Gaza's busiest souk, no IDF soldier would dare go alone very far into the crowd. The risk of being kidnapped or killed by a Palestinian mob would stop any but the most fool-hardy—or inexperienced—of the Israeli intruders.

I hate those dirty Jews! I can't wait to kill one someday. Panting, Sami slipped into an alleyway and stopped to catch his breath.

In January 1988, Sami Abbasi was well on his way to a life of violence. Prison was virtually certain, and an early death likely, but either would be a small price to pay for doing his part to get back Palestinian land and keep Israelis out of the Gaza settlements for good. Sami dreamed of being a part of the solution that would win for his countrymen the ongoing war with Israel once and for all. They would show the world. The nation of Palestine would soon be born!

"Sami, why did it take you so long to get home from school today?"

Miriam Abbasi crossed her arms as the boy walked in the kitchen door.

"You weren't throwing rocks at Israeli soldiers again, were you? You know our neighbor Nabil was hit between the eyes by a rubber bullet and almost died from it. He isn't much older than you. It's not worth it. Rocks are not going to solve this conflict, so stay away from the soldiers, Sami."

Although Miriam quietly appreciated her son's desire to fight Israel, she feared his death too much to encourage his zeal. Sami was already too much involved in the Intifada.[2] Rocks were bad enough to evoke Israeli rage, but she knew he had graduated beyond just stones. Molotov cocktails were far more deadly for "unarmed" combatants, and he had gained a reputation among his friends for strength and accuracy with his throws. Eventually, the reputation would be his undoing.

"Don't worry, Ami. I won't get caught. Our Palestinian people have suffered too much. When that Israeli army truck killed the family of four near Jabalia, I don't think it was an accident. The soldiers deliberately tried to run them down. Too many people witnessed it.

"Ami, how can I *not* help my people? For decades, others have seen the Israelis as underdogs, and people have felt sorry for *them*. But that view will change as we show the world Palestinians are the ones who suffer. The Intifada will make it clear." He looked in his mother's eyes. "Did you know the Israelis have publicly said they will 'break the bones of the Palestinian youth'?"

Sami folded his arms and sat down at the table. His father was not home yet, though, and he would have a tougher time convincing him that Sami should be one of thousands of Palestinian rock throwers.

Miriam pondered her son's serious face, appreciating his vision, but unable to release her fear for his well-being.

"Sami, why don't you express your rage by spray-painting graffiti on the barricades? Artwork is nonviolent, but it still gets the point across."

Sami chuckled. "Ami, I love you and thank you for wanting to protect me. But let girls do the graffiti. I must do something more for my people. One day, all of this will be over, and the flag of Palestine will fly above Jerusalem!"

"But you are only thirteen years old, Sami. At this rate, you won't live long enough to see your dream come true. Leave the fighting to the older boys—at least for now. I want to see you grow up, get married, and someday have several children." She grinned playfully. "How can I be a grandmother if you die?"

Miriam made her point the way she always did with Sami. She poured a large serving of guilt over him to clinch an argument. Sami smiled, stood up from the kitchen table, and headed for his bedroom.

An hour later, hairs on the back of Sami's neck prickled at the unmistakable grumble of tanks grinding the pavement several blocks away. Sami scrambled off his bed and climbed over the windowsill into the softening late-afternoon light. At the corner of the block, he met five friends, drawn to the street by the same passion that drove Sami. They dashed across the pavement to Gaza Baptist Church, their favorite cover near the Palestinian parliament. They scurried under a billboard-size portrait of Yasser Arafat and along the wall surrounding the church property.

As the sound of tanks faded, the boys clambered over the wall. Inside the compound, a dozen yards to their left, the church pastor was unlocking the heavy iron entrance gate. The man had seen them and, pocketing his keys, was already walking in their direction. It was Wednesday night, and soon the place would be packed for Bible study and youth group.

"Care to stay, boys, and join the fun tonight? We're having pizza." He smiled invitingly. "It's being delivered in just a few minutes."

Sami was shocked that Pastor Habib welcomed them instead of delivering a tongue lashing for their blatant act of trespassing.

"I'm Greek Orthodox." Sami searched for the right words. "And I'm, uh, not sure my parents would approve of my attending your meeting." Despite his cautionary response, Sami wanted desperately to go inside and see what the pastor's program was all about. His school friends had raved about the games, the food—and the cute girls at these Wednesday night meetings.

"Maybe next time, Pastor." Sami nodded a bit too forcefully. "I'll ask my parents and see what they think . . . And thank you for not getting after us for hopping over your wall." He pointed toward the barrier. "Tanks were coming, and we hid from them. We weren't breaking in or anything; don't worry about that!"

He cringed inside at the thought that he had overemphasized their innocence—which, of course, would make them seem anything but innocent.

"I'm sure you weren't, Sami." Pastor Habib extended a hand to the group spokesperson. "I trust you."

Sami raised his hand reflexively to meet the pastor's but was astonished at what he had just heard. "How did you know my name? Have we met before?"

"I've seen you around the neighborhood, and I asked a friend what your name is."

"Why would you do that, Pastor Habib?" Sami suspected a sinister side to this "man of God."

"Oh, I always like to know the names of people I pray for." He smiled. "Have a good night, boys. I hope to see you around."

A week after his first face-to-face meeting with Pastor Habib, Sami Abbasi was among the first to arrive for the youth meeting, excited to see that pizza was on the menu again. During subsequent weeks, Sami would discover that the Gaza Baptist Church served pizza every Wednesday night.

Although the teenager relished the all-you-can-eat spread,

he puzzled over the questions each Wednesday night Bible study raised in his mind.

Jesus told us to love our enemies? But that's impossible. Anyone in Gaza who loved Jews would be killed if it were found out. How could anyone love the Jews anyway after what they do to us Palestinians?

And where are all the other Arab nations who said they would send help? None of them are lifting a finger for us.

In the past six months, more than 160 Palestinians lay dead on the streets of Gaza and the West Bank, thanks to the Jews. How do we love that?

As the weeks passed, Sami's questions gradually drained the passion out of his vision for Intifada. Young people continued to lead the fight, but Sami's friends lost their star Molotov cocktail thrower.

Relieved that their son was less and less in harm's way, George and Miriam Abbasi encouraged Sami's visits to the Baptist youth group—as long as he attended Greek Orthodox services on Sunday. Although baffled by Sami's fascination with the Bible, if it kept him from throwing rocks at Israeli soldiers, the Abbasis weren't about to challenge him on it. Their priest was not so sure about the influence, though. He warned that a growing number of teens were leaving the church and said it was heresy that the Baptist church performed full-immersion baptism. One day during worship, he even told the congregation he had contacted PLO officials, and they would soon be investigating the Gaza Baptist Church.

A year after the Intifada began—and a month before Sami's fourteenth birthday—the Gaza Strip imploded. An Israeli hit squad assassinated PLO leader Khalil al-Wazir while in Tunis. He was known as Abu Jihad, the "Father of the Struggle," and his death triggered massive demonstrations in the Gaza Strip and West Bank and sparked internal retributions.

Palestinian youth by the hundreds joined indigenous organizations such as the revolutionary Palestinian Red Eagles and West Bank Black Panthers, who were intent upon finding "traitors" suspected of collaborating with Israel. When discovered—or sometimes just suspected—by these "special troops," the turncoats were brutally executed in public. Men hung upside down by lynch mobs became part of the scenery for even Palestinian children to see. The dark underbelly of the "freedom fight" too often provided cover for the settling of old family scores as some Palestinians accused of working with Israel were "surprisingly" found out, too late, to be innocent.

During this terror-ridden collapse of Gaza, now known as the *First* Intifada, Sami Abbasi made peace with God. His desire to kill Jews was replaced with a desire to live like Jesus. In his own words, he reflects on his experience this way:

The Intifada actually brought Muslims and Christians together. Before that, we lived as separate communities. But the conflict gave us a common problem: the Jews. We shared a hatred of Israel. But inwardly, I hated Muslims too! I blamed both them and the Jews for the prison state of existence we lived in.

When I read the Sermon on the Mount, though, it changed my perspective. I knew I had to find another path than hatred and violence. I decided the only way to follow Jesus was to be a full-fledged disciple. I could not pick and choose some of the things Jesus called His followers to do. I knew it was "all or nothing," and I decided all.

When I came to Jesus, I laid down my hatred when I embraced the cross and committed to love my enemies. Living in Gaza gives a person many reasons to hate, but at fourteen years of age, I gave them all up. Even though I didn't leave Gaza at the time, I became part of something much greater than building a Palestinian state. I was a part of a "state" where all people are welcome: the kingdom of God.

Nearly fifteen years later, in January 2002, Sami Abbasi readied himself for a visit to Yasser Arafat's mosque in Gaza City. Recently the center of the Israeli-Palestinian conflict, the mosque became Sami's target—not for rocks and missiles but to invade with the Rock of Ages. His bride was apprehensive about the new mission endeavor.

"We must not be afraid, Adelle. Jesus has called us to be His first responders in this crisis. Palestinian people are despondent now that President Arafat's home has been destroyed. The Israelis promised to level his house if he did not stop launching rockets into Israel, and now that they've made good on their promise, our Palestinian friends and neighbors are more miserable than ever."

"But Sami, why go down to the mosque—*his* mosque? What if the Israelis launch another strike? We both heard drones all night last night, and that usually means the next day IDF takes out another target." She reached for her husband's arm. "Who's to say it's not going to be right where you're standing?"

"I understand why you're worried, habibti, but you do realize that being by a mosque is actually the safest place in Gaza right now. Israel never destroys religious structures. Even in the Intifada, they have not bombed a single mosque. Arafat's mosque has not been damaged at all." He paused, reflecting.

"Did you know that it's a replica of the Dome of the Rock in Jerusalem?

"I saw on the news that Islamic students as well as Muslim imams are hanging out there, assuming it will be safe. And the people who live near the mosque are some of the poorest in Gaza. They're also ashamed that their president's home is a pile of rubble. Jesus preached good news to the poor, and I want to tell them that we ache with them. I want to bring Jesus' love into the chaos.

"Plus, two Americans staying with Pastor Habib want to visit with Muslims, and I'm the best one to be their 'tour guide.' It will surprise people at the mosque but open doors to talk with them. Muslims think all Americans hate them—you know, because of 9/11 and all the CNN coverage of people cheering in Gaza."

Sami wrapped arms around his wife's waist, pulled her close, and rested his cheek on the top of her head. "I promise to be here for dinner, my precious. Jesus will protect me. After all, I have to be home to grill the kabobs."

"I know a shortcut that avoids downtown."

Walid leaned back from the driver's seat of the Toyota taxi van and grinned at his passengers, a missing front tooth most likely the reminder of either an Intifada street brawl or a slightly more than fender-bender mishap driving the volatile streets of Gaza City.

"It's just a quick right off this street and then a left. Should save us at least fifteen minutes."

Sami, his ministry partner Ali, and the two Americans

with him in the back seats shifted onto each other when Walid wheeled the van into the side street. As the passengers righted themselves, all five men in the van gaped at the scene in front of them. Several hundred Palestinian men stood chanting in the street, black keffiyehs obscuring each face. Pounding drums supported the shouting crowd as effigies of George Bush and Ariel Sharon blazed at the front of the mob. Additional spectators cheered from rooftops and upper-story windows all along the block.

"Whoops!" Walid raised his eyebrows and cocked his head, attempting a humorous look. "I think we'll take the long way to the mosque."

The driver glanced sheepishly in the rearview mirror, then turned to look out the back as he shifted the van into reverse.

Sami raised his arms as if addressing an audience. "Welcome to Gaza!"

The laughter triggered by Sami's "welcome" lightened the mood of everyone in the van, so arriving at the mosque fifteen minutes later, all were anxious to share some joy with the miserable-looking people streaming out of Friday prayers at the golden-domed mosque. Most walked with their heads down.

As the foursome exited the van, Sami squelched the awkwardness he felt again as the two Americans stepped out wearing shorts—a naively inappropriate fashion among dishdashas, keffiyehs, and burqas. He paid Walid the fare, then turned toward the despondent Palestinians plodding along the street and began trying to make eye contact. Within minutes, his gently joyful approach to the strangers had changed the mood of most people the four men encountered, and he turned the Americans into useful props, posing them for pictures in front of the mosque with newfound friends. One devoted-looking man even slipped his arm around the waist of the American from Colorado for his photo.

The ad hoc meet-and-greet on the steps of the mosque brightened the day for several dozen Friday prayer attendees until a half dozen clerics stormed out the main door of the mosque, beards and white robes flapping in the breeze created by their swift movement. Brandishing Korans, the mosque leaders offered barely gracious greetings followed quickly by thinly veiled threats as to what would befall the four interlopers if they did not soon vacate the Arafat holy site.

As Sami tried to focus on the speaker's words, he noticed one of the men studying Sami's face and scribbling on a pocket-sized notepad. While the harangue continued from the mosque group leader, the man completed his observations of Sami and turned toward Ali. Even though he and Ali were obviously Palestinian, it was equally obvious they were not at the mosque to offer condolences over the loss of President Arafat's house.

Mohammad Khan stuffed the notepad under his robe and pulled out a cell phone. As an agent of the Islamic Resistance Movement—soon to be known worldwide as Hamas—his call precipitated a relentless scrutiny of Sami and his friends.

Four years later, undeterred by endless surveillance, intimidation, and few visible ministry results, Sami's work blossomed in October 2006. Through his church gone underground, he had discipled two Muslims who were following Jesus, and he explained again to his wife the significance of what he hoped was about to happen.

"Adelle, Muslims are open to Christ more than I have ever seen in my life. Do you know they are telling me about a new phenomenon? They're having dreams about Jesus! Why would these people tell me this?

"I believe it is simply the grace of God. Our Father in heaven knows my heart once overflowed with contempt for followers of Islam, but now, He has given me *His* heart for these desperate and misguided people. Muslims—the people—are not the problem. *Islam* is the problem, and its followers are the religion's victims."

Sami pointed across the bedroom at his wife. "Today, you and I need to meet with three couples who have reached out, asking me for spiritual direction. I've arranged a secure place, and from the way they approached me, I suspect they've *all* been having dreams about Jesus. I pray so!"

Adelle looked up at Sami from her seat on the edge of the bed. After being up most of the night with their one-year-old daughter, her ten-minute nap had not been enough to rejuvenate her. "Sami, I'm so tired. Mirna is still not feeling well, and I just don't think I can make it this afternoon."

"I promise, Adelle, we'll only be there for one cup of tea. Just one and no more."

The young woman sighed. "Okay, I'll ask your parents to watch Mirna."

A quarter of an hour later, Sami and Adelle caught a cab and headed to a nondescript apartment near the center of Gaza City. As he unlocked the front door, Sami explained to Adelle that this was a safe house the church could now use for small secret meetings but not large groups. Sami left the curtains closed, and the husband-wife team set about in the kitchen preparing tea.

An hour later, the three other couples had arrived. Other than courteous greetings at the door, no one spoke until the group settled into the dimly lit living room for tea.

Ismail Rantisi nodded at Adelle as she poured his tea, cleared his throat, and looked directly at Sami. "We want to follow Jesus." He glanced at Adelle and then back at her husband. "That's why we got in touch with you.

"I was flipping through TV channels one night, and Father Zakaria out of Egypt was on. The way he spoke to the imams who called in astounded me. He had remarkable answers for everything—answers to questions I'd had all my life about my religion. It floored me to think I might be wrong and that Islam might *not* be the correct path to God. *What if it was Jesus?* I thought. That night, I couldn't sleep, because the question wouldn't leave me.

"The next night was no better. So finally I prayed: 'Jesus, if You are the way to heaven . . . show me.'

"Right away, I drifted into a peaceful sleep for the rest of the night. But I wasn't prepared for what Fatima told me the next morning." He pointed at his wife. "She seemed uncomfortable during breakfast but finally said to me: 'Jesus came to me in a dream last night.'

"I wasn't quite sure what to think, so I simply asked her if He told her anything.

"Fatima suddenly looked radiant. She put her hand on her heart and said, 'Yes, He did tell me something, Ismail. I will never forget what He said.'

"*Whoa*, I thought. My heart was pounding in my chest. Now I was dying to know the message, and here's what she told me:

"'Jesus said He is the way to heaven and that I should tell you He said so. Ismail, He also told me that He loves us. Jesus said that He *loves* us! He knows our names. I cannot even imagine this. I have never felt so serene and loved in my life.'"

Ismail scanned the other faces in the room, then opened his hands in Sami's direction. "So, Sami, here we are, living in Jabalia Refugee Camp where the First Intifada began. The Uprising *began* in Jabalia, the only home any of us have ever known. We lived through it and survived—barely, but we survived.

"And now Fatima and I have had, I suppose, a spiritual intifada, an uprising of the heart, and we found out that we are not alone. Our friends have had similar experiences with Jesus." He shook his head. "Can you believe that? Jabalia is a hard place. The battles with Israel seem unending and don't look like they'll be stopping soon. But what makes us feel alone is that our Arab brothers in other countries don't help us. Where are the Saudis with all their riches? Where are the Jordanians? Why did Egypt refuse to take back Gaza when Israel offered it after they won the Six-Day War? Why does Syria not help us?

"The answer is that they don't care. *Nobody* cares about us—except Jesus. He even knows our names." Ismail looked at the other couples again, then focused his eyes on Sami. "We want to pray and give our lives to Him—*now*."

Sami swallowed the lump in his throat and took Adelle by the hand, then slid off the couch and knelt on the floor. The others joined him as he and Adelle led the six men and women in a prayer of commitment. Each prayed in turn, then Sami offered a final plea for blessing upon everyone gathered, but before he could say "Amen," the front window exploded, spewing glass on all eight people in the room.

"Hit the floor!" Ismail threw his arm around Fatima and pulled the kneeling woman the rest of the way to the tile flooring.

Bullets thudded into the wall above the couch on which Sami and Adelle had been seated before the prayer.

From his prone position amidst shattered glass, Sami recited scripture. "The reason the Son of God appeared is to destroy the works of the devil . . . Whoever has the Son has life; whoever does not have the Son of God does not have life."

What seemed to be a lone attacker rattled two more bursts of automatic fire into the house, then left the shaken couples in silence. The women wept softly as the four couples rose slowly from the floor and hugged each other. Saying little in the stunned aftermath of the attack, they walked solemnly through the kitchen to the back door. Two by two, they darted across the tiny yard behind the apartment building, climbed over a wall topped with barbed wire, and ran in separate directions.

Back at home, Sami and Adelle sank beside one another on their living room sofa. Sami's eyes drifted to the ceiling. *"Welcome to the body of Christ.* That's all I could think of, Adelle, when the bullets rained in. Enemies of Christ are everywhere in Gaza." He rolled his head to look at his wife. "How are you, my sweet? I'm so sorry to drag you into this situation."

Adelle said nothing but rested her head on Sami's shoulder. They sat quietly for several minutes before Sami pulled the cell phone from his pocket and punched in a number.

"Ismail, are you, Fatima, and the other four all right? Were you followed?"

The voice on the other end of the line was strangely exhilarated.

"Giving your life to Jesus sure comes with excitement, doesn't it? We didn't even finish our prayer before someone is trying to kill us. Who do you think it was, Sami? And how did he know where we were meeting?"

"You've got me, Ismail. So much for that safe house. We need to support one another, though. Let's meet again in two days. I'll have a new place by then. And remember: your lives are in Jesus' hands right now. He will protect and keep you under His covering. Look out for Hamas in Jabalia."

"I won't have to look far, Sami. My brother is a member."

Twelve months later, Hamas controlled the government of Gaza, and it seemed to Sami that the gates of hell had opened in Gaza when Hamas took power. Islamic Jihad and the Palestinian Authority still fought for control of the streets. Yet Sami's ministry—now joined by Ali, Rami, Ismail, and several other dedicated followers—seemed as on fire as many of the buildings in Gaza City. The Holy Spirit made His presence known to them daily. One morning over breakfast, Sami shared the latest example with Adelle.

"I had a dream last night that I think was from the Lord. He showed me a terrible battle raging in Gaza, and our apartment was caught in the crossfire. But we ended up being fine because angels stretched out their wings over us."

The next day, Hamas and Palestinian Authority fighters swarmed the Abassis' neighborhood, and buildings on every side of their apartment erupted with gunfire. A senior Hamas leader who lived down the street had become this week's number one target for the Palestinian Authority.

For the thirty-six hours of the gun battle, Sami and Adelle could not walk or stand upright in their apartment. Like a rainstorm, bullets sprayed the building in waves, interrupted by periodic explosions that rocked the entire structure. Sami and

Adelle crawled to the bathroom, the kitchen, and the bedroom. Adelle placed cotton in Sarah's ears and sang to drown out the sound of guns. Gaza was under siege, but "Amazing Grace" sounded from the Abbasi apartment as angels watched over the family.

Three months following the gun battle, a Muslim family in the neighborhood invited Sami for a visit. He had just settled into the Hajjars' living room for an evening of conversation when a son arrived home from an errand. The teen slumped through the room, to his bedroom, ignoring his parents and Sami. Several minutes later, though, the conversation turned in the direction Sami had hoped, and he mentioned the name "Jesus." The boy exploded from the bedroom, screaming obscenities and waving a claw hammer above his head, and charged at Sami.

Sami stood from the couch and shouted, "In the name of Jesus, stop!"

The boy halted as if he had hit a brick wall and simply stared at Sami.

"Ahmad?" His mother tried to get the boy's attention.

The teenager looked vacantly at his mother, then back at Sami. "Can you help me?"

Ahmad, the parents explained, had been violent since he was a young boy, for reasons no one could grasp. Whatever the problem—demonic or psychological—Sami assured them Jesus could help, and he read from the New Testament, calming the boy. At the end of the evening, the family invited Sami to come again, and within a few days, Ahmad and his parents had committed to follow Jesus.

The evening after the Hajj family came to Christ, Sami reflected with Adelle on the state of believers in Gaza.

"Rami Ayyad told me that he knows of some Muslims who are becoming brave enough to stop by the Bible Society of Gaza to ask for a New Testament."

Within a few weeks of his conversion, Rami Ayyad, one of the first disciples in Sami's Gaza Strip ministry, had begun working at the Bible Society of Gaza. With his newfound love of Scripture, he could think of no better place to spend his days than giving Bibles to anyone who asked for one.

Sami shook his head. "These are days we will never forget, Adelle. We're on the verge of something really big."

The coming changes were so big, in fact, that many powerful people were determined to stop them.

Rami Ayyad let the front door of the Bible Society office close softly behind him as he concluded his shift. A breeze rustled his hair in the October twilight. As he turned toward the street, a familiar car caught his attention. Even in the dim light, he recognized it—and its two occupants—as the vehicle that had been shadowing him for the past two weeks. Hairs on the back of his neck prickled as for the first time he noticed that the car had no license plates. He thought of Pauline. Pregnant with their third child, she would be anxious for him to arrive home tonight. Rami pulled the cell phone from his pants pocket and dialed the number for his wife. She picked up on the third ring.

"Pauline," Rami said as he glanced at the car, "if I am not home soon . . . I may not be seeing you for a while."

The words were the last Pauline Ayyad ever heard from her husband. The kidnapping ended in Rami's martyrdom.

Upon hearing of Rami's death, Sami went to the morgue to view his friend's body. He could not fathom that this brother in Christ was dead. He recounts the grief in his own words:

I was there when Rami committed his life to Christ. Gentle and soft-spoken, his smile would light up a room, and in spite of death, his life will speak for years to come. He had told all of us that we should expect persecution and even said the Lord showed him that one of us was going to die.

Rami was discovered, facedown, in the street a few days after his last shift at the Bible Society. The people who found him said that when they turned his body over, Rami was smiling. I know he was with Jesus—Rami Ayyad, the first Palestinian martyr for Christ, our version of the apostle Stephen.

Hamas denied involvement in Rami's death, yet the claim is suspicious, at best. In 2007, at the time of his death, the organization had begun a publicized crackdown on any suspected religious activity that wasn't in line with fundamentalist Islamic ideology. Mohammad Khan had been gathering evidence against Sami, Ali, and others involved in Muslim outreach. And to add to the fear permeating the Strip, Abu Saqer, a high-ranking Muslim, accused leaders in the Gaza Christian community of "proselytizing and trying to convert Muslims with funding from American evangelicals" and promised heavy retribution for their "crimes."

Sami continues the story.

I have lived around Muslims my whole life. I'm used to their threats, but Hamas took all of it to a new level. Authorities end-lessly interrogated some of our new disciples. Yet we saw miracle after miracle in the Gaza Strip!

Take Jalil, for instance. Fearless in sharing Jesus with other Muslims, he had been a believer for only a few months before he was arrested and put in jail. Knowing what he would face, we asked the Lord to keep him strong. A few other new believers had been broken through interrogations and beatings, and sadly, some even converted back to Islam. They do that out of fear, to appease their families, or to keep their jobs. But not Jalil!

The second night of his lockup, Jalil dreamed that God sent an angel to open his jail cell. Remembering the story from Acts when Peter and John were freed from prison by an angel, Jalil took heart and felt prepared for the next day of questioning—and probable beating.

But it never happened! The next morning, a guard paced nerv-ously back and forth by Jalil's cell and stopped several times in front of it, as if trying to decide what to do. Finally, he looked through the cell door at Jalil and smiled. Without a word, he took out his key, opened the cell, and motioned for Jalil to leave.

Jalil told four Muslim friends about his miracle escape that day. It was so obviously of the Lord that soon Jalil was discipling all four of them.

Mohammad Khan and his fellow Hamas operatives ramped up their surveillance and became intentionally obvious—just to intim-idate us, I suspect. Since I was undoubtedly on the Hamas hit list, other ministry leaders begged me to leave the Gaza Strip until the situation cooled down.

I was reluctant, but the week before Christmas 2008, Adelle, little Mirna, nine other families, and I headed through the Erez

Crossing on our way to Bethlehem. I cried leaving the people I loved and confess that Adelle and I were worried about the new Muslim Background Believers. I would now have to disciple them by phone.

Still, our ministry with Muslims continued. The West Bank is not as crowded as Gaza, and many of the Muslim villages there are unreached. But our life in the West Bank opened an unexpected new opportunity. For the first time ever, I met Jewish people face-to-face. The closest I'd ever come before was close enough to throw rocks at their Jeeps. I was in my mid-thirties before I actually met a Jew.

Although I gave up my hatred for Jews when I became a disciple of Jesus, I have to admit that I was constantly fighting to not let hate for Jews seep back into my heart. News services in Gaza fed the temptation. They never publish anything remotely complimentary of the Jewish State, and it was hard not to swallow the poison. Every time I felt hostility rising in my heart, though, I confessed it to God. Jesus did not call any of us to a life of hate.

In the West Bank, I met Aaron, the son of an Orthodox rabbi in Jerusalem. With his long side curls, black hat, and prayer tassels peeking from under his knee-length black coat, he could have been a "poster boy" for Judaism. He was even involved in government affairs related to the Orthodox Jewish community in Israel.

The prestige of his family in Jerusalem assured that Aaron's future was thoroughly planned for him: He would spend his life in study and prayer, know all the rabbinical interpretations of the Torah, and pursue academic knowledge of all things Jewish—yet Aaron felt empty and lifeless. He thirsted for a vibrant relationship with God and had tired of tradition and duty. That's when God arranged for Aaron and me to cross paths.

The first miracle was that I even made it to Jerusalem. A person from Gaza is not supposed to travel outside the Strip, but we received *permission from the Israeli government because of Hamas's persecution of Christians.*

So here I was, a Palestinian from Gaza, drinking coffee in Jerusalem's Aroma coffee shop, surrounded by Jews. I felt like I was in a scene from a movie when Aaron spotted me reading the Bible and asked to sit with me.

I must have looked at him like he was from another planet. I noticed that Aaron glanced around the coffee shop after every question he asked. He was deeply frightened but began asking questions about Jesus.

"Sami," he told me, "I have many more questions for you. But we cannot meet in public. It's too dangerous. Everyone knows me here. I'm getting looks just for visiting with you right now. Can I have your number, so we can arrange a place later today? I must visit with you. It's urgent!" Aaron appeared to be having a panic attack as he scribbled my number down and left.

As I told Adelle later, that meeting with Aaron was like talking with a modern-day Nicodemus. My heart broke for him. He seemed so religious yet terrified of what other Jews might think of his having a conversation with me. I was not prepared for what happened, though, when we met late that afternoon at Aaron's chosen safe spot, the Jerusalem Forest.

"Sami!" Aaron caught sight of his target at the trailhead and trotted past several parked cars to join the man from Gaza. "Thank you for meeting me in the forest."

He glanced over both shoulders and waved his hand in the direction of the trail, indicating that they should begin walking. "It was the only place I could think of where we would not be watched. In Aroma, I saw you reading your Bible, and I noticed it was the New Testament. It was obvious you were an Arab, and I guessed at something else."

Aaron touched Sami's right arm and the two men stopped, just far enough down the trail to be invisible from the parking area.

Aaron smiled. "The way you looked while reading told me."

Sami cocked his head, curious.

"The peace was obvious on your face, and you looked toward heaven while you thought about what you had just read. I knew you had to be a believer."

Sami startled as Aaron grabbed him by both shoulders and looked him in the eye. "Sami, you are the first brother in Christ I've ever met! I'm a Jesus follower too."

Sami gaped at Aaron as the Jewish man wrapped his arms around Sami and lifted him off the ground.

Slowly grasping the situation, Sami hugged Aaron back. "I thought you wanted to know more about Jesus. It never occurred to me that you might already be a believer! Wow!"

The two men found a picnic bench and sat down together.

"I thought about reading the New Testament for a while, but I never got around to it." Aaron shook his head. "It bothered me that Jews would bash Jesus, yet they didn't really seem to know anything about Him. They never had a dialogue with Jewish believers. Instead they just yelled at them. I didn't like Christians—or Jewish believers either—but I thought the Jewish arguments against Christianity were based on old myths.

"So I decided to find a copy of the Christian Bible, so I could answer the Messianic nuts who hang out in the Old City. How delusional I thought they were! Everyone knows the disciples stole Jesus' body, right? The whole resurrection thing was a big fraud.

"But before I got hold of a New Testament, I was walking through the Jaffa Gate in the Old City one day about six months ago, and a man handed me a piece of literature. At a glance, I could see it had something to do with religion and read the twelve scripture verses featured on the front page. I told him, 'I've never read this because I'm not allowed to read the New Testament. This is clearly about Jesus. I'm sorry—not interested,' and I tried to hand the tract back to him.

"That's when I got the surprise of my life. The man looked at me and said with warmth I really appreciated, 'Friend, this isn't from the New Testament.' He flipped the page over and there it told the source: Isaiah, chapter 53!

"I can't tell you what this did to my mind. It was like the Jaffa Gate collapsed on top of me. I was speechless, and I'm sure the man saw the effect it had on me. *How could I have missed reading this all my life?* I wondered. *This was in* our *Bible.*

"The man was so gracious. He could tell I was struggling with this revelation, but all he said was, 'Maybe you'd like to read some more. Since you mentioned the New Testament, here it is! My number is on the back. Call when you have questions. I'm sure you'll have plenty.'

"That day began my journey. I devoured the New Testament and kept it hidden in my closet in a pair of shoes. My wife knew nothing. She thought I was just studying the Torah late at night and was happy that her husband was so zealous about the Bible. She mentioned it to me at breakfast a few times, but she didn't know I was reading *the other Bible!*

"After several months, I was ready to follow Yeshua, the Jewish Messiah. I planned to give Him my life one night as I sat in the living room after everyone was asleep. I thought about what a joy it had been to read the New Testament; I'd been through it twice.

"I read Paul's words: 'If you declare with your mouth, "Jesus is Lord," and believe in your heart that God raised him from the dead, you will be saved.'

"As I started to say, 'Jesus, I'm ready,' my father walked in the front door unexpectedly and asked what I was reading.

"I told him the truth, and he started yelling at me. He blasted me for a couple of hours. That's when I realized how tough my road would be, but it didn't stop me.

"His verbal assault woke up the whole house, and I started getting questions from my wife, my mother-in-law—even a next-door neighbor joined in!

"They finally calmed down, but I didn't change my mind. When I went to bed that night, I prayed and asked the Jewish Messiah to forgive my sins.

"That's my story, Sami. I am privileged to meet you, brother. Who says Jews and Palestinians can't get along, right?"

Encouraged by his new friend's transparency, Sami shared his own story, confessing the long-time hatred for Jews and one-time desire to kill as many as possible. He asked Aaron for forgiveness, and Aaron, too, repented of his own hostility toward Arabs. They spent the rest of the afternoon in the forest, reading Scripture and discussing Aaron's long list of questions.

As they walked back to their cars for the trip home, Aaron made a request. "Sami, I need prayer, and I need encouragement. It's incredibly difficult to live among Orthodox Jews, and I'm not sure what the future holds. I need help. Would you mentor me like Paul did Timothy?"

That night at dinner, Sami recounted for Adelle the re-markable meeting with Aaron.

"Adelle, Aaron wants me to disciple him, but it's almost too much for me to take in right now. I feel as close to Aaron as I did to the Muslim Background Believers in Gaza—even though he's a Jew. This is such a gift from the Lord!" Sami threw his head back and looked for several seconds at the ceiling before continuing.

"Adelle, do you suppose it could possibly be that Jesus called us out of the Gaza Strip specifically so we could tell *the Jews* about Jesus?"

A WORD FROM SAMI

That is exactly what the Lord has called us to do. We now reach out to the Jews of Israel as well as to Muslims.

When I lived in Gaza, I saw the fence between the Strip and Israel every day and viewed it as a symbol of hatred between people. But I had my own barriers.

The first that God knocked down was the one in my heart between Muslims and me. How I detested them. But then God led Muslims like Ismail and the three couples to me, and I began to see them through Jesus' eyes. Now I've discovered that in the West Bank, Muslims here are interested in knowing Jesus. They are tired of religion and politics—aren't we all?

The second barrier, of course, was between Jews and me. Even though as a follower of Christ, I had committed to not hate anyone, I still didn't like Jews or anything connected with the State of Israel. When I saw a story on TV about Jews, I felt pain for my people. The conflict since 1948 is an ongoing nightmare for Palestinians. Both sides have legitimate claims, and the problems seem unsolvable. When I met Aaron, though, I saw him through Jesus' eyes as well. Aaron, too, was tired of religion and politics, and he wasn't "just a Jew." He was my brother in Christ.

I had a third barrier, though, that I didn't recognize until the Holy Spirit pointed it out. It was a barrier between hope and me. I had lost hope that the Palestinian–Israeli crisis would ever be solved. Then God took me into the forest to meet with Aaron, and I saw the answer. Our mutual commitment to Jesus erased all barriers. I ask you a question: Have you lost hope? If so, this is not the life that Jesus has for you. He *is our Hope.*

It was an honor to disciple Aaron. A Palestinian from Gaza training a Jew from Jerusalem on how to follow Jesus is hard to believe, right?

Aaron meets regularly with a group of Arabs and Jews who love Jesus. It's hard to imagine that such a group exists in Jerusalem, but the message of Jesus' reconciliation is spreading. It is the only possible way to bring Jews and Palestinians together.

Every time we meet, new Jewish believers ask Palestinians to forgive them for the hatred they harbored toward them. And Palestinians do the same with their Jewish brothers and sisters. It's amazing to think the conflict between Jews and Arabs goes back to Isaac and Ishmael and that the battle has been going on for 4,100 years.

Because of my relationship with Jews, I'm learning Hebrew. A Palestinian who communicates the love of Christ to Jews in their heart language will be especially meaningful. Pray for me, though, because this language is difficult.

One day in Jerusalem, I met an Orthodox Jewish man and told him I was from Gaza. I said it was a blessing to meet him, and the comment blew him away. So I told him that Jesus, the Jewish Messiah, replaced my hate and gave me love for Jews. He didn't seem to believe me, so I gave him my phone number and asked if we could get together. I said I would like to be his friend.

That night he called me to say he had told his family about meeting me, and they thought he was lying. So Moshe invited me over to the house right then and there. I joined them for a Sabbath meal! While there, I had the chance to tell his whole family about our wonderful Jesus. I told them Yeshua is our true Sabbath rest. Since I was their guest, they couldn't leave and wouldn't throw me out, but I don't even think they wanted to.

Adelle and I sense daily that God's hand of favor is on us. He has changed our course dramatically since we left Gaza. Maybe God has called you to a new assignment as well. Jews and Arabs joining in solidarity for the kingdom of God and seeing them pray and worship as one always makes us cry. Jesus has called Jews and Arabs in Christ to serve Him together. This is deep within the heart of God—and it is the real Jerusalem Peace Plan.

I used to run from Jews. Now I run to them. God has called me, a humble Palestinian, to reach the lost sheep of Israel. What an honor! Pray for my family, pray for me, and pray for the peace of Jerusalem!

Shalom-Salaam!

CONCLUSION

My previous book, *Killing Christians: Living the Faith Where It Is Not Safe to Believe*, focused on believers who were willing to die for their faith in Christ, many of whom did. *Standing in the Fire: Courageous Christians Living by Faith in Frightening Times* focuses on believers who are willing to die for their faith in Christ yet still live.

Like Shadrach, Meshach, and Abednego in the flames, the believers you've met in this book have no earthly reason to still be alive. King Nebuchadnezzar's fiery furnace is long gone. But the Islamic State and other terrorist groups use swords and crosses to torture and kill today. No other group of people could be more vilified by Islamic terrorist groups than Christians and specifically former Muslims who have committed their lives to Jesus like your new friends in *Standing in the Fire*.

So how do these saints of God thrive in the midst of Islamic terrorism and persecution?

I've consistently observed three spiritual disciplines inherent in each of these believers. Think of them as "tactics" that need to be employed during wartime. The first discipline was hammered home to me while ministering in Jordan.

SPIRITUAL DISCIPLINE #1—CHOOSE
WHAT VOICE YOU LISTEN TO

The church was packed in the ancient city of Jerash. The pastor stepped to the microphone and as if on cue, the mosque next door began blaring the Islamic call to prayer. I later learned that it actually was on cue.

"That happens every time we meet as a church," Pastor Maher shared with me later. "The muezzin climbs up the minaret and prays or makes announcements and blasts them at full volume to try to drown us out inside the church. He does this until we are finished meeting." Pastor Maher seemed completely unfazed by the interruptions that the faithful had endured for years.

I found it hard to fathom teaching the Bible, praying, or doing anything during the obnoxious interruptions. I opened in prayer and could barely get a cohesive request out of my mouth. "Why don't you move the church?" I blurted out the obvious.

"We don't need to. We've learned to deal with it and we're staying right where God has planted us." Maher then told me their technique for *muting the mosque.*

"*It's up to us to choose what we listen to.* It took practice and we had a lot of it, but we focus on what we want to hear, not the interruptions. That way we listen to what God has to say to us and not the noise that tries to block it out."

Pastor Maher summarized well the very heart of this book. *Standing in the Fire* was written to encourage you as a believer in Christ to live by faith in frightening times.

First Takeaway: ***It's up to you to make a choice as to what voice*** *you will listen to today.* The modern-day saints of God in this book would never be able to thrive in places like Syria, Iraq, and Gaza if their worldview came from the news and circumstances around them. Their stability comes from God's Word, radical obedience to Jesus, and dependence on the Holy Spirit's leading. Then they tune out the rest of the noise around them.

To live by faith in frightening times it's essential to tune out the noise around that chips away at our faith on a daily basis. As followers of Jesus, it will only be well with our soul if we allow the One to whom we have given our life, to control our equilibrium. Spiritually we must put on some noise cancellation headphones to tune out the ambient noise around us. Only God's view of the times we live in matters.

SPIRITUAL DISCIPLINE #2—
MAKE FAITH YOUR FILTER

My wife, JoAnn, just shared a Christine Wyrtzen devotional with me recently that leads us to our next point:

> Our pastor has been taking us through various Psalms this summer. Every single one, so far, has had to do with some facet of worry. Today, he said this. **"Faith is a filter."** That caught my attention because faith is the opposite response to anxiety. Faith reminds me (in the face of everything that concerns me) that God is ruling when it appears mayhem prevails, God is watching when I fear He's lost interest, God is active when I see no evidence of it, God is omniscient and I

am not, God is sovereign over all surprises, God is redemptive when life seems full of wasted pain, God is fiercely protective when His children are vulnerable, God is just when evil temporarily prospers, God is a faith-giver when I'm running on empty, and God is a Father who is never fatigued, distracted, nor disinterested. *"Let faith arise."* (from ChristineWyrtzen. com, devotional for July 4, 2016)

Second Takeaway: *Faith is your filter to screen out the world's pollution that can rob your soul of the peace that Jesus promised to all of us who love Him. Is faith your filter? Or is it worry? Air filters in a car need to be changed every so often because they get dirty. Maybe you need to throw your filter out. It's something we have to do not just once but often. So the next time you hear something disturbing on the news or something that affects you personally, remember this: "Worry is my old way of thinking. Our loving God is still on the throne, and He hasn't vacated His responsibilities as the Creator and Sustainer of the universe. The next time a trial or the news sends a jolt of adrenaline through you that could result in hours of worry, remind yourself—God's got this one."* Remember, as believers in Christ, we're victors not victims.

Pretty simple, right? Send everything through the filter of faith, not the filter of worry. Paul said we have to adjust our thinking this way: *"Since, then, you have been raised with Christ, set your hearts on things above, where Christ is, seated at the right hand of God. Set your minds on things above, not on earthly things. For you died, and your life is now hidden with Christ in God. When Christ, who is your life, appears, then you also will appear with him in glory"* (Col. 3:1–4 NIV)

SPIRITUAL DISCIPLINE #3—GET ON YOUR FACE AND PRAY

A popular app today to use for communication is called FaceTime. But believers who were determined to receive an answer from God have been getting on their faces for centuries. That's real "face time."

Anne Graham Lotz, in her excellent book *The Daniel Prayer*, speaks directly to our hearts as we face the fact that today America is unraveling morally, politically, and spiritually, right before our eyes. Anne's book shook me up and woke me up. It's refreshing and insightful, and she perceptively links America to the fall of the nation of Israel and its subsequent captivity. Anne wrote: "It didn't take long for Daniel; in the desperate situations he faced, to discover the power of God through prayer. Because God was all that Daniel had. Again and again he threw himself upon God with such complete faith and utter dependence that God came through for him. Powerfully. Personally. Dramatically. Repeatedly." (Anne Graham Lotz, *The Daniel Prayer* [Grand Rapids: Zondervan, 2015], 16)

Thank you, Anne!

Third Takeaway: **Prayer *still* moves mountains. It's time to get on our faces before God.** This may shock you, but I have learned more about praying in the last few years from former Muslims who are new believers in Christ than I have from most seasoned Christians. Talk about having enemies! Their own Muslim family members often want to kill them. When they pray, they are desperate. Are you? It's time for desperate praying.

Want to Get More Involved? Here are three ways you can help believers who are serving Christ faithfully in the Middle East's fiery furnace:

1. **Pray for them.** 8thirty8 on Facebook gives up-to-the-minute SOS prayer requests from the front lines daily. If you "like it" you'll receive updates daily and always be in the prayer loop with believers who are in prison, persecution, and danger. (www.facebook.com/8thirty8/)

2. **Serve with them.** We're not kidding. e3 Partners hosts mission trips to places where some of the people you read about in this book are serving. Ready to go? Just send an inquiry to: Phoebe4peace@gmail.com and we will train you, and then get you on the field to work with one of our teams. e3 will screen all applicants to make sure they are legit.

3. **Support them.** Interested in helping a national leader financially? We can get you connected, and you will be the one who is truly blessed. (www.e3partners.org/standing-in-the-fire)

Standing in the Fire was an honor to write. My wife, JoAnn, and I have learned much by sitting at the feet of those who live inside the furnace that has enveloped the Middle East. They live all-out for Christ every day because they may not have a tomorrow.

But let's not forget. Even though our circumstances are quite different, we're all *standing in the fire*. We may not be currently being killed for our faith in the Western world, but the persecution of Christians is at an all-time high. It's growing and spreading. Can we realistically say it will not reach us? It will.

Take a lesson from this new generation of believers in the Middle East who are rock-solid firm in their faith in Christ. They are unshakeable and refuse to run away by giving into their fear no matter how hot the furnace is heated. And it's getting hotter.

The times we live in are frightening, but we are right on course with the very plan of God for this world. *Things are not falling apart . . . they're falling into place.*

If you've given your life to Christ, you're not alone. You never were. You can face anything in life without being paralyzed by fear. Many of the new friends that you've met in this book are former Muslims. Now that they love Jesus, their lives are lived in constant danger. Yet even as new believers, they are willing to die for Jesus.

So this begs the question: Am I willing to *live* for Him? If you truly want to live all-out for Christ in today's world, you will experience blowback like never before. Since the whole world lies in the power of the evil one, as John the apostle tells us, why should we expect anything less?

But take heart, have courage, stand firm, and don't run away in fear. After all, Jesus is right there next to you—*standing in the fire.*

—Tom Doyle

ACKNOWLEDGMENTS

Thank you:

JoAnn Doyle for being the love of my life, and for so passionately bringing Jesus' love to women of the Middle East.

To the Doyle Tribe—Shanna, Tommy, John-Mark, Lindsay, Josh, and Sarah—I'm so proud of you and honored to be your dad. To the married-ins—Nora, Matt, and Travis— how thankful JoAnn and I are that you're part of our family.

To the Grands—Emma, Ethan, Emmet, and little Bennett—you're the apples of our eyes and joy of our hearts.

Back to you Josh Doyle—thank you for introducing me to Azzam, the Pirate of Somalia. His story in *Killing Christians* blew people away from the first page and it inspired many to live with courage.

Joel Rosenberg—for being a dear friend and for giving me the title of the book over dinner in Jerusalem.

Alexa Rearick—for your heart for God and for creating a powerful book cover. Thank you e3/I AM Second Creative.

David Shepherd and Greg Webster—I love being a team and I thank God for your friendship.

The HarperCollins Team—you are the best and you have become family.

The MECA Team, e3 National Leaders, and e3 Partners—what a joy it is to serve Jesus on the front lines with all of you.

The 8thirty8 Prayer Team—your faithful intercession in real time for our brothers and sisters in prison, persecution, and danger is moving the hand of God and connecting believers all around the world.

NOTES

CHAPTER 1: THE SYRIAN FIRING SQUAD

1. A geographic region including lands surrounding the eastern rim of the Mediterranean Sea.
2. A strict Islamic school that stresses memorizing the Koran.
3. An affectionate term by which a wife might address her husband; roughly the equivalent of "my darling."
4. A facial veil that leaves the eyes, upper cheekbones, and bridge of the nose exposed.
5. An Arabic word meaning "crazy."
6. The Hajj is the pilgrimage to Mecca that every Muslim is required to make at least once in his or her lifetime.
7. Feminine form of *habibi*.
8. An Arabic term meaning "Welcome!"
9. A Muslim prayer acknowledging Allah as the one true God and Muhammad as his prophet, translated roughly as, "There is no god but Allah. Muhammad is the messenger of God."

CHAPTER 2: THERE'S NO PLACE LIKE HOMS

1. We told an earlier story of Farid and his fellow believers, "The Only Empty Graveyard in Syria," in our previous book, *Killing Christians*.
2. The ancient city of Homs. See 2 Samuel 10 for the account of King Hadadezer.

3. The promontory on which the castle Krak des Chevaliers is built.
4. Muslim Background Believers.
5. 2 Corinthians 1:8–10 esv.
6. An Arabic term of affection between male friends.

CHAPTER 3: MARRIED TO AN IMAM

1. Friday prayers.
2. An Arabic gesture suggesting "this comes from my heart."

CHAPTER 4: THE MUSLIM WOMAN AT THE WELL

1. Arabic for "Mom."
2. An Arabic expression approximating "Good God!"
3. An Arabic expression meaning to take responsibility for something.

CHAPTER 5: JUST THE USUAL DAMASCUS DEATH THREAT

1. Arabic for "daddy."
2. A popular brand of Syrian-made cigarettes.
3. See Acts 9:11.

CHAPTER 6: THE ISIS RECRUIT FROM MOSUL

1. The mosque "pulpit" from which an imam preaches.
2. Arabic for "trial, affliction, or distress."
3. Punishments mandated under Sharia law.
4. Excerpted from English translation of Abu Bakr al-Baghdadi's Mosul address on July 4, 2014, posted at https://ansaaar1 .wordpress.com/2014/07/05/new-caliph-abu-bakr-al-baghdadi -%E2%94%82-english-preview-%E2%94%82-islamic-state-of -iraq-sham/. Accessed 6/29/16.
5. An Arabic acronym for "The Islamic State of Iraq and the Levant."
6. Non-Muslims living permanently in areas under Islamic government.

7. This is the testimony of Mosul Christians I interviewed in Jordan.
8. Kurdish military.

CHAPTER 7: THE SECRET POLICE SECRET

1. Taqiyah: an Islamic skullcap; dishdasha: long-sleeve, ankle-length garment similar to a robe.
2. Arabic for "Father of."
3. Syrian secret police.
4. A chemical weapons attack near Damascus on August 21, 2013.
5. Arabic for "Thank you."
6. Jordanian Dinar. One JD equals approximately $1.40 in U.S. dollars.

CHAPTER 8: THE JERUSALEM PEACE PLAN

1. Israel Defense Forces.
2. An Arabic word for "uprising" of the Palestinians against the Israelis.

ABOUT THE AUTHORS

Tom Doyle pastored churches in Colorado, Texas, and New Mexico for twenty years, and his involvement in the Middle East began with leading Bible Tours to Israel, Jordan, and Egypt. He eventually became a licensed tour guide in Israel. Along the way, Tom and his wife JoAnn fell in love with the people and soon it became clear that God was calling them to do something risky—to get involved. They jumped into working full-time in the Middle East just a few months before 9/11—a game-changing event for America and the Middle East. Tom now serves as the Vice President and Middle East Director of e3 Partners, a global church planting ministry. JoAnn is also with e3, and leads Not Forgotten, which is e3's Middle East women's initiative. Tom is the author of eight books, including *Dreams and Visions* and *Killing Christians*. The Doyles have six children and four grandchildren, and hopefully many more on the way!

Greg Webster is cofounder of New Vantage Publishing Partners, a book development and marketing firm, and creative director of Webster Creative Group. The collaborator of more than a dozen books for a variety of authors, including Tom Doyle's previous books *Dreams and Visions* and *Killing Christians*, he holds an MA in theology from Fuller Theological Seminary and a BA in journalism and an MBA from the University of Georgia. He lives and works in rural Tennessee, just outside Nashville, with his wife of thirty-six years and the four of his eight children who have not yet left the nest.

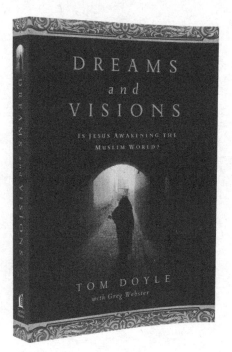